Paul Bottalla

The papacy and schism

strictures on Mr. Ffoulkes' letter to Archbishop Manning

Paul Bottalla

The papacy and schism
strictures on Mr. Ffoulkes' letter to Archbishop Manning

ISBN/EAN: 9783741193163

Manufactured in Europe, USA, Canada, Australia, Japa

Cover: Foto ©Lupo / pixelio.de

Manufactured and distributed by brebook publishing software (www.brebook.com)

Paul Bottalla

The papacy and schism

PREFACE.

THE following pages would never have been written had not the author been urged to undertake the task by persons to whom deference was due. He is sensible that it is late to take the field against Mr. Ffoulkes, when the essays of Dr. Ward and Father Ryder have been so long before the public; but these answers, masterly as they are in themselves, deal chiefly with the doctrinal questions involved, and do not enter fully into the erroneous views of history which occupy so large a part of the notorious pamphlet. The present writer has accordingly addressed himself mainly to the historical points; at the same time he has travelled so far into the region of dogma as to point out how incompatible with the Catholic profession is the defence of the English Establishment which Mr. Ffoulkes has attempted to set up.

Gold is refined in the fire, and the more

virulently truth is attacked, the more is her unchanging endurance manifested. The task of the writer has been laborious. His labour will be abundantly repaid if he lead any to see that the Catholic faith stands ever firm, and is proof against the efforts of all open enemies or insidious friends.

TABLE OF CONTENTS.

PREFACE . . . pp. vii., viii.

I.

Prejudice and ignorance renew old calumnies against the Catholic Church. Mr. Ffoulkes' Letter affords an instance of this. His fundamental errors against Papal power already refuted in another work . . . . pp. 1—4.

II.

That the False Decretals were forged at Rome is now an exploded error. The Code of Justellus is not the Code of the Canons of the fifth century, much less the Code binding on the whole Church. Great mistake of Mr. Ffoulkes. Progress and development of Ecclesiastical Legislation. Collection of Dionysius: its character . . . . . pp. 5—13.

III.

Canonical authorities recognised in the ninth century. Pope Nicholas, while pointing out the true sources of ecclesiastical legislation, does not mention the False Decretals. True character of the controversy between that Pope and Bishop Hincmar. Mistake of Hinschius. The grounds on which Pope Nicholas rests his Papal prerogatives are identical with those urged by his predecessors. For two centuries the False Decretals were generally neglected by the Popes. They produced no change in connection with the authority of the Pope in the Church. They merely insisted on maxims which were already admitted . . . . . pp. 14—26.

IV.

The appeal to the Pope in cases of importance did not originate from the False Decretals. True meaning of the Canons of Sardica. Innocent I., Leo I., Gregory I. on this subject. Code of Justinian. Words of Ebediesu on the authority of the Popes over the Patriarchs . . . pp. 26—32.

V.

The See of Rome, in virtue of its divine institution, the supreme Court of Appeal in the Church. Testimonies of the elder Popes upon the subject . . . . . pp. 32—36.

VI.

Twofold object of the Decrees of Councils. No need to define the Papal supremacy before it was attacked. The doctrine clearly conveyed by the Canons of Sardica. The Ninth Canon of Chalcedon in perfect harmony with those of Sardica. Appellate jurisdiction of the Patriarch of Constantinople compared with that of the Pope. Papal Decretals binding all over the Church . . . . pp. 37—47.

VII.

Serious mistake committed by Mr. Ffoulkes in quoting Father Régnon's Articles on the False Decretals. The doctrine of the latter stands in perfect opposition to the principles of the former. Opinions of Hinschius and of Father Régnon on the discipline introduced by the False Decretals concerning the judgments of Metropolitans. No new discipline on that matter first originated by the False Decretals . . pp. 48—55.

VIII.

No fault imputable to the Popes for not having ascertained the spurious character of the False Decretals. They acted in this matter with great prudence and reserve. The quotations from the Decretals do not in any way affect the doctrine or discipline of the Church. Examination of a passage quoted by Mr. Ffoulkes from the Roman Catechism on the Sacrament of Confirmation . . . . . . pp. 55—61.

xi

IX.

Contradictory ideas held by Mr. Ffoulkes on the subject of the Crusades. It is untrue that the Crusaders completed the aggrandisement of the Papacy. Mr. Ffoulkes misunderstands Catholic unity. Neither the Crusaders nor the Popes entertained any project of becoming masters of Constantinople. The history of the capture of that city. Cruel conduct of the Greeks towards the Crusaders. Innocent III. and the Crusades . . . . pp. 61—72.

X.

Election of Thomas Morosini to the Patriarchal See of Constantinople. Conduct of John Camater the Greek Patriarch. The False Decretals in no connection with the election of Morosini. This election was perfectly canonical . . pp. 72—78.

XI.

Vain attempt of Mr. Ffoulkes to apologise for the Anglican schism. It was not a revolt against any spurious legislation in the Church, but against a divine authority, which had been acknowledged for centuries. Patriarchal rights of the Pope over England. The Eighth Canon of Ephesus in no way opposed to this. Both the Anglo-Saxon and the British Churches were subject to the Pope from their first origin. The protest attributed to the British Prelates in the age of St. Augustine is a mere forgery. Historical facts in confirmation of the original submission of the British Church to Rome . . . . pp. 78—91.

XII.

False colour given to the Greek schism by Mr. Ffoulkes. No doctrinal difference led the Greeks to their separation from Rome. Sketch of the principal circumstances which brought them to schism. The right of Rome to the universal supremacy was always acknowledged by the Eastern Church down to the age of Photius and Cerularius. The addition of the word *Filioque* no cause of the schism, much less the Pseudo-Decretals or the prerogatives claimed by the Popes . . . . pp. 91—105.

STRICTURES,

ETC.

I.

MEN of this nineteenth century are accustomed to boast of the prodigious progress that has been made in historical criticism, and in those positive studies which tend constantly to dissipate more and more effectually the prejudices and to disprove the calumnies of past times. It is then not a little startling to meet with an author of our own day, who has been bold enough to maintain the astounding paradox, that the authority of the Popes, and their supremacy in the Church, was established only by force and fraud. Still more astounding is it to be told, when we ask what is the judgment of history on the point, that it "replies with clearness and sternness in this very sense." Assertions like this are frequent in books and periodicals written in the interests of Protestantism; they prove nothing except the ignorance of history which still prevails among certain classes; for history is the pure mirror which receives the light of former ages and reflects it on our own.

Every now and then the old and oft-refuted calumnies of the Centuriators are once more brought into light, changed in form rather than in substance, and paraded as the results of recent research and modern criticism. This is just what Mr. Ffoulkes has done in the works which have lately brought his name prominently before the world. The volumes on *Christendom's Divisions* make no small display of historical erudition, but the author writes as a man of the sixteenth century, and seems unconscious that any advance has been made since that time in critical studies. The same peculiarity of mind is seen in the *Letter to Archbishop Manning;* its pages are found to contain an incredible number of blunders, and give proof of a really remarkable absence of critical spirit, and even, at times, of a mental gift that is less rare. Presuming that this pamphlet fairly displays the powers of the author's mind, we have the consolation at least of seeing how he may be more excusable with reference to his errors and heresies, than at first sight might appear. Here is—in Mr. Ffoulkes' own words—one result of his investigations into universal history. He tells us that, "History deposes, in short, unhesitatingly, that Rome rose to the eminence which she occupied in the thirteenth century . . . by fraud and force . . . the most striking specimens of each kind being the Pseudo-Decretals, including of course the pseudo-donation and the Crusades. By these means her Bishop aspired to become a Patriarch of the whole Church, as well as a Pope."[1]

Now the history of eighteen centuries protests

---

[1] *The Church's Creed, or the Crown's Creed.* A Letter to the Most Rev. Archbp. Manning. By E. S. Ffoulkes, B.D. London, 1869. Pages 26, 27.

against this passage. Mr. Ffoulkes should have known this, for he has been many years a Catholic, and he was induced to become one through his study of history. If he entered the Church upon historic rather than divine faith, and if he has read himself out of his convictions, he should have left the Catholic Church. But he maintains that he is still a Catholic : although the divine institution of the supremacy of the Pope is *of faith*, nor could he honestly have become a Catholic without accepting this tenet as a part of the revealed Christian doctrine. Further, the only branch of ecclesiastical science to which, as far as we can learn, he has given any special attention, is that of Church history. He tells us too, that before coming to his latest conclusions, as set forth in his recent pamphlet, he made full inquiries into the subject, comparing document with document and communion with communion. And yet it seems, that throughout the course of his researches he has never lighted on any of the original and authentic letters of early Popes, nor has even had his notice attracted by any of those events in the history of the first ages of the Church, which display the supremacy of the Popes complete in all its features, acknowledged in theory and exercised in practice, centuries before the publication of the False Decretals.

Original authentic Letters still exist in which early Popes declare to the world that to them has been entrusted by Christ the care of all the Churches. This is undeniable. In a work lately published, *The Supreme Authority of the Pope*, several passages to this purport will be found collected into a few pages;

extracts are given from the letters of twelve Popes before the time of St. Gregory the Great, who, as is also proved, held the same view as to the extent and nature of the Pontifical prerogative.[1] We may be permitted to refer to the testimony of a critic who certainly has but little sympathy with any claims of Church authority, but who asserts that by this collection of passages the Anglican High Church party are defeated on their own ground.[2] In the same work abundant proof is given of the steady exercise of the universal power claimed by the Popes, and which they grounded upon the promises and commission given by Christ to St. Peter. In those days no question was raised as to the legitimacy of the Papal claim; it was admitted in principle even by those who from time to time refused to render the obedience which they did not deny to be due.[3]

Mr. Ffoulkes should not be ignorant of the existence of this body of evidence, and what has he found to put forward in opposition? His whole argument is based upon the False Decretals, with the pseudo-donation of Constantine, and the Crusades.[4] A short examination, however, into the subject will show how insufficient is this statement for proof of his theory.

[1] *The Supreme Authority of the Pope*, sec. iii., pp. 63—69.
[2] *London Review*, Sept. 2, 1868.
[3] *The Supreme Authority of the Pope*, secs. iv., v., pp. 81—138.
[4] *The Church's Creed*, &c., p. 27.

II.

First, then, as to the False Decretals. Men of the Reformation era might be excused for expressing doubt whether or not the False Decretals were fabricated at Rome, or by the orders of Rome, but since that time deep and conscientious study has been devoted to the subject, and the result is, the almost unanimous agreement of writers who have made themselves capable of forming an opinion. They tell us that the Isidorian Collection was not manufactured at Rome or by the orders of Rome. The contrary has indeed been maintained within the last forty years by Theiner and Eichhorn; their exceptional view does not hinder the harmony and agreement of all other authors; while some of the leading scholars of modern Germany have employed themselves in thoroughly refuting the arguments by which these two writers were misled.[1] This is not the place to go fully into the subject; it will be sufficient if we quote the words with which Hinschius concludes his discussion: "When everything is weighed, it is abundantly certain that the Decretals had their birth in France."[2] The same result was arrived at long ago by Ballerini, whom Hinschius not unfrequently quotes.[3] We are excused from going further into the matter by the conviction which Mr. Ffoulkes expresses, that even if the Pseudo-

---

[1] See the last and the most learned of all P. Hinschius' works, *Decretales Pseudo-Isidorianæ*, pt. v., sec. 22, cap. i., p. cciv., seq. Lipsiæ, 1863.

[2] *Ibid.*, p. ccviii.

[3] Ballerini, *De Antiq. Collect. et Collect. Canonum*, pt. iii., cap. vi., sec. iv. (Opera S. Leonis, t. iii., p. ccxxii., seq. Venetiis).

Decretals were not manufactured at Rome or by order of Rome, "for all that, Rome stands committed to them no less than if she had done both." The writer enlarges on this point for eight pages consecutively, crowding into them a multitude of historical blunders, some stated broadly and others implied. We will review them in order. First, in spite of the appearance of great erudition so conspicuous in this writer's pages, he seems to know nothing of the sources and historical development of ecclesiastical jurisprudence. The year 1869 is indeed a very late one in which to be told "that the 'Code of the Universal Church' was in existence, as a Collection, at the time of the Fourth Council, is established by Justellus and others *indisputably*, . . . and therefore it is unquestionably binding on the whole Church still, and always has been."[1] For persons who know anything of the results of recent studies in ecclesiastical history, this passage is alone sufficient to show how wholly incompetent is Mr. Ffoulkes to handle the subjects of which he has presumed to treat. The question is, whether it be true that since the time of the Synod of Chalcedon, a Code of the Universal Church has existed binding on the whole Church then and now; and whether it be true that this Code was the one published by Justellus in 1610. Such a fiction may have been credible two or three centuries ago, and so we may find some excuse for Justellus, and two or three others who agreed with him.[2] But at

[1] *The Church's Creed*, pp. 27, 28.
[2] Christopher Justellus published in Paris, in 1610, this supposed Code of the Canons of the Universal Church, under the title of *Codex Canonum Ecclesiæ Universalis, a Conc. Chalcedonensi et a Justiniano confirmatus.*

the present day we smile when we read such a statement, and the more as it is made by a man who pretends to sit in judgment on the Church and on the Popes. Scholars had unanimously, long before our own time, been awakened from this dream. David,[1] Florens,[2] Coustant,[3] Berardi,[4] Ballerini,[5] and other learned writers, have long, long ago put this question to rest. The blunder of Justellus was like that into which Quesnel fell, when he tried to persuade the public that the old Gallican collection of Canons was the *Codex Canonum Ecclesiæ Romanæ*, belonging to the sixth century. But Justellus, when challenged to produce a manuscript of his collection, in order to justify his publication, was unable to exhibit any which contained exactly what he had given to the world. He had borrowed portions from various sources, published and unpublished, in order to enrich his collection, and he had no ancient authority whatever for the pompous title given to his volume—*Code of the Universal Church.* Mr. Ffoulkes does not betray the smallest suspicion that this title was manufactured by Justellus himself. He seems to consider that he gives an irrefragable proof of the genuineness of the Collection when he points out that the Canons cited in the Fourth and Eleventh Sessions of the Fourth General Council answer exactly to the numbering which they bear now in the publication of

---

[1] *Des Jugements Canoniques des Evêques*, cap. ii., p. 55, seq. Paris, 1671.
[2] *Diss. de Origine art. et Auct. Juris Canonici* (Op., t. i., p. 27).
[3] *Epistolæ Rom. Pontif.*, Præf., sec. i., n. 53, p. 58.
[4] *Gratiani Canones genuini*, Præf., p. 8, seq.
[5] *De Antiq. Coll. et Coll. Can.*, pt. i., cap. vi., n. 2, p. xxxiv., seq.

Justellus.¹ But, simple man, is it possible that he is not aware that Justellus himself arranged the numeration of his own Code in such a manner as to make the numbering correspond to the quotations in the Council, although no manuscript is in existence which lends any countenance to this arrangement.² Moreover, how could Mr. Ffoulkes believe that the Code of Justellus was binding on the Universal Church when, among the other Canons of Chalcedon, it contains the Twenty-eighth,³ which Mr. Ffoulkes professes not to admit, on the ground that it was never confirmed by Rome?⁴ But this is not all. If Mr. Ffoulkes believes that no Canon could have authority without the consent of the Pope, he cannot consistently maintain that the Code of Justellus was the authoritative Code of the Universal Church before the Council of Chalcedon. For, in the first place, that Code contains the Canons of Antioch,⁵ which had been rejected by Pope Innocent I., and denounced by him as an invention of heretics, which should not be inserted among the Catholic Canons.⁶ Again, the Code contains the Canons of the first

---

[1] We wish to attribute to a misprint, that Mr. Ffoulkes refers the first two quotations of Canons lxxxiii. and lxxxiv. to the Ninth Action of the Council of Chalcedon, when they belong to the Fourth (See Labbe, *Conc.*, t. iv., p. 1427. Edit. Venet.).

[2] See Ballerini, Op. cit., pt. i., cap. i., n. 7, p. viii., seq.

[3] *Codex Ecclesiæ Univ.*, edit. cit., p. 124, seq.

[4] *The Church's Creed*, p. 28.

[5] *Codex Ecclesiæ Univ.*, p. 44, seq.

[6] Innocentius I., *Epist.* vii. *ad Clerum Constantinop.*, n. 3 (Coustant, p. 799). "Nam quæ ab hæreticis sunt excogitata Catholicis regulis adjungere non licet." David (Op. cit., cap. ii., art. v., p. 94, seq.) shows from documents which he adduces that many of the Oriental Prelates spoke with contempt of these Canons.

Council of Constantinople,[1] and who does not know that Leo the Great distinctly refused to acknowledge those Canons?[2] Who, moreover, is now unaware that St. Gregory the Great declares that, in his age, the Canons of Constantinople were not yet acknowledged and received in the Church?[3] On the contrary, the Canons of Sardica, which the Roman Church fully sanctioned, did not find their way into the *Code of the Universal Church*. Mr. Ffoulkes, then, is ready to receive a Collection as the Code of the Universal Church which, on his own principles, he must admit to contain Canons rejected by the authority of the Church, and yet to exclude Canons admitted by the Church as the rule of its discipline. We leave to our author to explain this glaring contradiction.

The fact is, that before the Council of Chalcedon a collection of Canons existed which at first comprehended only those of Nicæa, Ancyra, Neocæsarea, and Gangra; but before the Council was assembled, the Canons of Antioch and of other Synods had been added to it;[4] the Canons of Ephesus were not added until the sixth century, and yet they are found in the collection which Justellus pretends was in use in the middle of the fifth. But that collection had no sanction from the Church, and therefore no public authority. In fact, not only Innocent I. in the Letter which we have quoted, but St. Chrysostom himself, and the Bishops

[1] *Codex Ecclesiæ Univ.*, p. 86, seq.
[2] *Epist.* cvi. *ad Anatolium*, cap. v. (Edit. Ballerini, Op., t. i., p. 1166).
[3] *Epist.* l. vii., *Epist.* xxxiv. (Op., t. ii., p. 882. Edit. Maur).
[4] See on this subject Ballerini, Op. cit., pt. i., cap. ii., n. v., p. xiii.; Coustant, Op. cit., Præf., n. 53, seq., p. lviii., seq.

of his party, when pressed with the Fourth Canon of Antioch, which had already found a place in that Code, refused to admit its authority, because they asserted, as Pope Innocent I. had done, that these Canons of Antioch had been enacted by the Arians.[1] But whatever authority the Code of the Oriental Church may have had in the East, certainly it was not received by the Latins till about the sixth century. Up to that time the only Canons sanctioned in the Roman Church were those of Nicæa, with the supplemental legislation of Sardica; for the Council of Sardica was always regarded in antiquity as an appendix to that of Nicæa. And this explains the reason why the Sardican Canons are inserted among those of Nicæa, and are called by the same name. Innocent I., in his Letter to Theophilus, Patriarch of Alexandria,[2] expressly declared that the Roman Church did not admit other Canons than those of Nicæa. In another Letter addressed to the Clergy and people of Constantinople, he not only insisted on the same principle, but added in a solemn manner that the Canons of Nicæa were the only Canons which ought to be admitted throughout the whole Catholic Church.[3]

---

[1] Socrates, *Hist. Eccl.*, l. vi., cap. xviii., p. 327 (Edit. Valesii, Moguntiæ); Sozomenus, *Hist. Eccl.*, l. viii., cap. xxvi., p. 795 (Edit. cit.).

[2] *Epist.* v. *ad Theophilum Alex. Episc.* (Coustant, Op. cit., p. 790). "Siste te ad Synodum quæ secundum Christum fuerit, et ibi expositis criminationibus sub testibus Nicæni concilii Canonibus (alium enim canonem Romana non admittit Ecclesia) securitatem habebis contradictionis expertem."

[3] *Epist.* vii. *ad Clerum et populum Constantinop.*, n. 3 (Coustant, Op. cit., p. 799). "Quod autem ad canonum observantiam attinet, solis illis parendum esse dicimus, qui Nicæni definiti sunt; quos solos sectari et agnoscere debet Ecclesia Catholica."

Of course when he spoke thus he did not mean to exclude the Canons of Sardica which were embodied in the Collection of Nicæa, even in several Codes of the Oriental Church, where their authority was recognised.[1] But we can undoubtedly assert that until the Collection of Dionysius appeared, no Code of Canons existed which was officially acknowledged by the Roman Church. Whenever the need of a new rule was felt, the Roman Pontiffs legislated by their Decretals; the originals of which were preserved in the Papal Archives, in order to verify when necessary the authenticity of the law.[2] That these Pontifical Decretals had full authority in the Church, clearly appears not only from what we read in the Epistles of Celestine I. and Leo the Great,[3] but also from what Dionysius says in the Preface to his *Canonical Collection*.[4] But when the latter published his *Collection*, which comprehended the Canons as well as the Papal Decretals, it met with general favour in Italy and elsewhere, although it was not complete in every part.[5] It was then that the Roman Church began to use it, quoting by name those Decretals, of which the originals existed in the Papal Archives.[6] It did not however receive any formal, unequivocal sanction from the Roman Pontiffs. It is true that some additions were made to the *Collection*

---

[1] See Ballerini, Op. cit., pt. i., cap. vi., n. 14, p. xli.

[2] See Coustant, Op. cit., Præf., n. 44, p. xlv. seq.

[3] Cœlestinus I., *Epist.* v. *ad Episcopos Apuliæ et Calabriæ*, n. 1 (Coustant, Op. cit., p. 1072); Leo M., *Epist.* iv., cap. v. (Op., t. i., p. 616).

[4] *Codex Canonum Ecclesiasticorum*, Præf. (Migne, *PP. LL.*, t. lxvii., p. 141, seq.).

[5] See Ballerini, Op. cit., pt. iii., cap. i., n. 6, seq., p. clxxviii., seq.

[6] *Ibid.*, p. clxxx.

by Pope Hadrian, who afterwards offered a copy of the whole to the Emperor Charlemagne; but nothing was done which could avail to give sanction to a mere private compilation. Nor was the adoption of the Code by the National Synod of Aix-la-Chapelle sufficient to impress upon it any new character of authority, even though the *Collection* was called simply Codex Canonum, or Codex Hadrianus.[1] It is true that some time in the course of the ninth century the Code came to be regarded practically as comprising the Canon Law in force in the Roman Church. The reader will find the proof of this hereafter; but it does not appear that this quasi-official character was given to it by any public act of Pope or Council.[2]

We have said enough to point out to Mr. Ffoulkes the course of study he should have adopted before he ventured upon the assumption that the *Collection* published by Justellus was the real Code of the Universal Church, having force of law at the time of the appearance of the False Decretals. Had he made himself acquainted with his subject before writing upon it, he would not have blamed Catholic apologists for omitting to consider the "palpable contradiction between the latter and the Canons of the whole Church, which the Pope was bound to uphold and enforce." It is true that nothing has been said upon this contradiction by those who have written in defence of the Papal prerogatives.

[1] L. c.
[2] Cassiodorus, who lived towards the middle of the sixth century, bears solemn witness to that custom. "Quos," he says, speaking of the Canons of that Collection, "hodie usu celeberrimo Ecclesia Romana complectitur" (*Divin. Litterarum*, cap. xxiii., Op., t. ii., p. 522. Edit. Venetiis, 1729).

But then, they were in no way called upon to reconcile their views of the teaching of antiquity with a Code of Canons which was conceived in the fertile brain of Justellus about two hundred and fifty years ago, and which owes its present restoration to fame only to the strange mistake of Mr. Ffoulkes.

Mr. Ffoulkes would wish his readers to believe that the argument which we have just been considering has never been answered, because it is unanswerable! We believe we have said enough to show that it has not been answered because it has never been thought worth answering. It was difficult to believe that Justellus' compilation could still obtain credit from any one. But the argument admits of another direct and full answer. There is no contradiction whatever between the doctrine concerning the Papal prerogatives contained in the False Decretals, and the *Jus Ecclesiasticum* of the Universal Church in the nineteenth century. We shall hereafter prove this assertion at some length. But we will at once show that it is nothing short of a calumny for a scholar of the present day to affirm that the forgery of the Pseudo-Isidore was the foundation on which the edifice of the Papal supremacy was erected.

III.

No doubt can any longer be entertained that the False Decretals were first circulated about the year 852 or 853. This result has been arrived at after elaborate researches by many learned critics, Catholic and Protestant.[1] From what source then did the Roman Pontiffs of that date consider that the Canon Law binding on the whole Church was to be derived? The documents still remaining to us furnish a clear answer— namely, the great leading maxims given to the Church by her Divine Founder, and consigned to Scripture or to Tradition, held the first place. The second rank was given to the Canonical authorities as contained in the so-called Hadrianic Collection, in which the authentic Decretals of preceding Popes were comprised. As to these Canonical authorities, we have an evident proof in the two following extracts from Epistles of Popes Leo IV. and Nicholas I. The former, in his Letter to the Bishops of Britain, decrees as follows: "It is not proper to judge any one by *libelli* and commentaries of others, putting aside the Canons of the Councils and the rules of the Decretals, which are now in our Archives, together with the Canons, and which we use in all the ecclesiastical judgments. They are the Canons of the Apostles, of Nicæa, of Ancyra, of Neocæsarea, of Gangra, of Antioch, of Laodicea, of Chalcedon, of Sardica, of Carthage, and of Africa, and moreover the Decretals of the Popes Sylvester, Siricius, Innocent,

---

[1] See Ballerini, Op. cit., pt. iii., cap. vi., sec. iv., p. ccxxiii., seq.; Hinschius, *Decretales Pseudo-Isid.*, pt. iv., cap. ii., p. clxxxvi., seq.

Zosimus, Celestine, Leo, Gelasius, Hilary, Symmachus, Simplicius. These are indeed the principles according to which the Bishops judge, and by which both Bishops and Clergy are judged. That if a new and extraordinary case should arise, for the determination of which the above rules were insufficient, then should you remember any maxims laid down on the subject by St. Jerome, St. Austin, St. Isidore, or any other holy Doctors of the Church; these are the guides whom you must follow; or the case should be referred to the Holy See."[1] Pope Nicholas I. also, in a Letter to Hincmar of Rheims, A.D. 863, authoritatively laid down that in ecclesiastical causes nobody should dare to pronounce any judgment except in accordance with the Canons of Nicæa, and of the other Councils, and in agreement with the Decrees of the Roman Pontiffs Siricius, Innocent, Zosimus, Celestine, Boniface, Leo, Hilary, Gelasius, Gregory, and others, saving the right of the Apostolic See.[2] From these expressions we gather the views of Pope Nicholas regarding the sources of the Canon Law by which the Church was governed. At the time when he wrote, the False Decretals had already made their appearance in France, and were spreading and gaining acceptance in

---

[1] *Epist.* ii. *ad Episcopos Britanniæ*, n. vi. (Labbe, t. ix., p. 1027).

[2] Nicolai I., *Epist.* v. *ad Hincmarum Episc. Rem.* (in *App. Epist.*, Labbe, t. ix., p. 1507). "Sancimus ne quilibet . . . impune audeat seu valeat aliena expetere aut expectare judicia, aut alienas contra canones ordinationes suscipere, vel ad alias provincias irregulariter convolare, sed ita ut Nicænorum et cæterorum Conciliorum canonicis definitionibus est promulgatum, et beatorum Siricii, Innocentii, Zosimi, Cœlestini, Bonifacii, Leonis, Hilarii, Gelasii, Gregorii ac cæterorum Romanæ Sedis Pontificum constitutionibus est decretum, salvo in omnibus jure Apostolicæ Sedis."

all directions. Yet the Pope makes no allusion whatever to these Decretals, nor does he in any degree rest upon them in claiming authority over the whole Church, or settling points of discipline;[1] but he repeatedly quotes the genuine Canons of early Councils and the authentic Decretals of his predecessors.[2] Lupus, an Abbot of Ferrara, wishing to know whether an alleged Decretal of Melchiades was authentic, applied to the Pope for information.[3] Nicholas could not find the original in the

[1] We must lament the mistake made by Dr. Hefele, when he asserted that Pope Nicholas had quoted a false Decretal of Pope Julius in his Epistle to King Charles the Bald (*Epist.* xl., in Conc. Rom. vii., penes Labbe, t. ix., p. 276). Dr. Denzinger pointed out the error in his *Ecloge et Epicrisis eorum quæ a recentioribus criticis de Pseudo-Isidorianis Decretalibus statuta sunt* (penes Migne, *PP. LL.*, t. cxxxiii., p. xii.). We think it certain that the passage quoted by Dr. Hefele from Pope Nicholas' Letter is merely a summary of what is said in the *Historia Tripartita*. But, moreover, Pope Nicholas must have had in mind the genuine Letter of Pope Julius to the Orientals when he wrote as follows—" Sed et Papa Julius Orientalibus scribens utramque partem, Athanasii scilicet et adversariorum ejus accelerare præsentiam, quatenus utraque parte præsente audiretur reus et ab omnibus condemnatus, de cætero cohiberetur a sacerdote." Pope Julius, in his Letter (penes Coustant, *Epist.* i., n. 21, p. 383), says—" Quod si arbitramini posse quædam adversus illos probari, et coram eos convinci, veniant quibus id placuerit . . . ut præsentibus omnibus, qui rei sunt convincantur, nec ulterius perturbatio in Ecclesia existat." Pope Nicholas, though not intending to quote the exact words of Julius I., refers to the Letter which is quoted above. Hinschius holds the same opinion upon this point (Op. cit., pt. v., sec. 22, cap. i., pp. cciv., ccv.).

[2] In proof of this we could here allege nearly all Pope Nicholas' Letters. See, for instance, *Epist.* ii. *ad Michaelem Imp.* (Labbe, t. ix., p. 1293); *Epist.* viii. ad eundem (Labbe, l. c., p. 1323, seq.); *Epist.* iv. *ad Adventum Episc.*, in Append. (Labbe, l. c., p. 1506); *Epist.* xl. *ad Carolum Calvum*, et xlii. *ad Univ. Episc. Galliæ*, in Conc. Rom. vii. (Labbe, t. x., p. 275, seq., et p. 281, seq.).

[3] *Scriptum Servati Lupi, Abb. Ferrariensis* (Labbe, t. ix., p. 1530).

Papal Archives, and therefore abstained from answering the question; but he abstained also from using the doubtful authority when himself writing to Wenilo, on whose behalf Lupus had made his application.[1] And yet the subject was one which might have naturally led the Pope to make use of the Letter of his predecessors, and to be guided by it in his own conduct.

While touching upon this subject, a few remarks will not be irrelevant upon the controversy between Pope Nicholas and Hincmar, Archbishop of Rheims. Whoever reads with care the Letter addressed by Nicholas to the Bishops of France in 863, will see clearly that the Pope does not in any manner recognise the authenticity of the False Decretals, nor give them any sanction, much less does he rest his claim to authority upon them. At this date, no doubt whatever of their authenticity was entertained by Hincmar, who ascribed the Collection to Isidore Mercator. This is proved by a letter which he wrote three years later to King Charles the Bald, in which some portion of the False Decretals is quoted in support of the liberties of the Church,[2] and also in the book which he wrote in 870 against the work compiled by his nephew in the Synod of Altigny. In that work Hincmar not only acknowledged the authenticity of the False Decretals, but alleged them in several instances, in order to produce proof of contested and fancied rights of the Episcopate.[3] The controversy between

---

[1] *Epist.* xxiii. *ad Venilonem Arch. Senon.*, &c., in App. (Labbe, l. c.).

[2] *Expositio* i. *Hincmari Rem. ad Carolum Regem* (Migne, *PP. LL.*, t. cxxv., p. 1042, seq.).

[3] See *Opusc. et Epist. Hincmari Rem. in causa Hincmari Laudunensis*, capp. xxiv., xxv., xxvi. (Migne, *PP. LL.*, t. cxxvi.,

C

Nicholas and Hincmar related exclusively to the question whether Papal Decretals which had not found a place in the Collection of Hadrian could be considered as having any authority in the Church.[1] The Pope maintained that Decretals possessed an inherent authority, altogether independent of their insertion in, or omission from, any Collection whatever;[2] and he established his position by arguments drawn from Scripture, Councils, Decretals which had been admitted into the Hadrianic Collection, and lastly, from the inconveniences which would attend the adoption of the principle upheld by his opponent.[3] He never once made appeal to the False Decretals in order "to prostrate at his feet the one great Transalpine Prelate who could still maintain the independence of the Teutonic Church," as Milman boldly asserts him to have done.[4] The Transalpine Prelate was aiming at an enlargement of the authority of the Metropolitans by adopting Canonical principles like those which, later on, became part of the Gallican system,[5] and on this account Pope Nicholas resisted

p. 377, seq., p. 384, seq.). It was only in 872 that Hincmar of Rheims began to object to the authenticity of the Decretals, in a letter written in the name of King Charles the Bald to Hadrian II. (It may be seen in Migne, *PP. LL.*, t. cxxiv., p. 896).

[1] "Quidam vestrum scripserunt, haud illa Decretalia priscorum Pontificum in toto Codicis canonum corpore contineri descripta," &c. (*Epist.* xlii. *ad Univ. Episc. Galliæ.* Labbe, t. x., p. 282).

[2] L. c.

[3] L. c., p. 282, seq.

[4] *Hist. of Latin Christianity*, vol. ii., bk. v., ch. iv., p. 303. Edition of 1857.

[5] See the work of Hincmar against his nephew, especially capp. x.—xix. (Migne, *PP. LL.*, t. c., p. 316, seq.). We are sorry that Hinschius, following the opinion of Wasserschleben, entertains the idea that Pope Nicholas I., in his Epistle to all the Bishops of

and checked his encroachments by the power of his Pontifical authority.

But let us examine more closely the ground on which that great Pontiff rested his supreme authority at a time subsequent to the propagation of the False Decretals. Milman again,[1] and Mr. Ffoulkes, maintain that not only does the Roman See owe to that Pope and his successors the vast moral advance of the Popedom, but also its supreme authority itself, by the

---

France on the cause of Rothad, had adopted the principles of the Pseudo-Decretals with reference to episcopal causes (Op. cit., pt. 5, sec. 22, cap. i., p. ccv., seq.). But we cannot believe that the Pope derived from these forged letters a right, which was then in full vigour. In fact, he appeals to the Letter of Pope Leo I. to Anastasius of Thessalonica (Labbe, t. x., p. 281, in Con. Rom.); he quotes in support of his view the letter addressed by the Sardican Council to Pope Julius (*Ibid.*); he again appeals to the authority of Leo I. and Innocent I. to prove that no difference should be made between the causes of the Metropolitans and those of Suffragan Bishops, since all are equal in Order though not in Jurisdiction (*Ibid*, p. 284). Finally, he discusses the question upon its intrinsic merits, and shows that the causes of the Bishops truly belong to the category of the *Causæ Majores*. With these proofs before us, how can any one affirm that Pope Nicholas endeavoured to increase his power and jurisdiction by the use of the False Decretals? Nor can it be asserted that in his Letter to Salamon King of the Bretons—which he wrote three years before the latter, and before knowing, as is said, of the Pseudo-Decretals (*Epist.* xxii. Labbe, t. ix., p. 1527)—he had held quite different principles. Because in this Letter he had in view a totally different object. In it he states what is required by the Canon Law that an ecclesiastical tribunal may be legally constituted and authorised to judge and condemn a Bishop. But in the Letter above mentioned he maintains that a sentence of deposition pronounced against a Bishop by a lawful and competent tribunal, should not be carried into execution without the sanction of the Pope. These two statements are in no way contradictory.

[1] Milman, l. c.; Ffoulkes, l. c.; and *Christendom's Divisions* pt. ii., ch. i., p. 53, seq.

sanction he gave to the False Decretals, as if they were the law of the Church. Historically this is a gross mistake; dogmatically it is a heresy. Pope Nicholas, no less than all his predecessors, derived his supreme authority simply and solely from the institution of Christ. This truth is more apparent from the Letters of Nicholas the Great than from those of any other Pope. Thus, in his first Letter, which is addressed to the whole Catholic world, he bases his claim upon the words whereby Christ appointed Peter to be Universal Pastor, and bestowed upon this Apostle the office of confirming his brethren.[1] In doing this he used no other language than that which had been familiar to his predecessors Boniface I.,[2] Leo I.,[3] Gelasius,[4] Gregory the Great,[5] Agatho,[6] Hadrian I.;[7] all of whom lived and wrote long before the False Decretals were ever heard of. Again, Pope Nicholas makes exactly the same use of the promises of Jesus Christ to St. Peter, in the

---

[1] "Quo audito (sicut a Deo inspirata vestra novit prudentia) cunctarum Christi ovium cura constringimur, cum vices ipsius gerimus, cui specialiter divinitus dicitur: 'Pasce oves meas.' Et iterum: Tu (inquit) aliquando confirma fratres tuos; non potuimus dissimulare, non potuimus negligere, quominus visitaremus oves dispersas et dissipatas, vel quominus confirmaremus in fide et bonis moribus fratres nostros et proximos" (*Epist.* i. *ad Univ. Catholicos.* Labbe, t. ix., p. 1289).

[2] Bonifacius I., *Epist.* v., nn. 1, 2 (Coustant, p. 1022).

[3] Leo I., *Sermo* iv. *De Natali ipsius* (Op., t. i., p. 19. Edit. Ball.).

[4] Gelasius, *Epist.* v. (Labbe, t. v., p. 298).

[5] Gregorius M., *Epist.*, l. v., p. 20 (Op., t. ii., p. 748. Edit. Maur.).

[6] Agatho, *Epist. ad Constantinum Pogon.*, in Act. iv., Conc. Œc. vi. (Labbe, t. vii., p. 654).

[7] Adrianus, *Epist. ad Tarasium*, in Act. ii., Conc. vii. (Labbe, t. viii., p. 747).

Letter which he wrote to the Emperor Michael,[1] read in the Eighth Ecumenical Synod and inserted in its Acts,[2] and also in that addressed to Photius,[3] to which also the same Council refers.[4] Peter is constituted the Rock; to Peter the keys are committed; and from this the Pontiff deduces the consequence that the Papal authority comprises all Christians whatever, no exception being admissible.[5] The like use had been made of the same promises by a long series of preceding Popes, as by Zosimus,[6] Boniface I.,[7] Celestine I.,[8] Leo I.,[9] Simplicius,[10] Gelasius,[11] Gregory I.,[12] Hadrian I.[13] Quotations to this effect could be greatly multiplied, showing that Pope Nicholas and his predecessors agreed in considering that the Papal authority rested on the sure basis of the divine promise and commission. And this alone is amply sufficient to show that the False Decretals were not the instruments by means of which the Popes were able to establish their sway over the

---

[1] *Epist.* ii. *ad Michaelem Imp.* (Labbe, t. ix., p. 1291).

[2] Conc. Constantinop. iv., Act. iv. (Labbe, t. x., pp. 530, 806).

[3] *Epist.* vi. *ad Photium* (Labbe, t. ix., p. 1303).

[4] Conc. Constantinop. iv., Act. iv. (Labbe, t. x., p. 539).

[5] "Et ideo consequens est ut quod ab hujus sedis rectoribus plena auctoritate sancitur nullius consuetudinis præpediente occasione proprias tantum sequentes voluntates removeatur; sed firmius atque inconcusse teneatur" (*Epist.* vi. *ad Photium.* Labbe, t. ix., p. 1304).

[6] *Epist.* xii., n. 1 (Coustant, p. 974).

[7] *Epist.* xv., n. 4 (Coustant, p. 1041).

[8] *Epist.* iii. *ad Episcopos Illyrici* (Coustant, p. 1064).

[9] *Serm.* iv. *De Nat. ipsius*, nn. 3, 4 (Op., t. i., p. 19. Edit. Ball.).

[10] *Epist.* iv. *ad Zenonem Imp.* (Labbe, t. v., p. 98).

[11] *Epist.* xiii. *ad Episc. Dardaniæ* (Labbe, t. v., p. 326), et in *Comm. ad Faustum* (l. c., p. 297).

[12] L. c.

[13] Epist. cit., in Act. ii., Syn. vii. (Labbe, t. viii., pp. 763, 764).

whole Church. We will give another argument. For two centuries after the first appearance of the False Decretals, they remained neglected by the Popes, and apparently almost unknown to them. With the exception of one or two quotations by Hadrian II. and Stephen IV., no one of the Roman Pontiffs before the middle of the eleventh century, paid any attention to the Pseudo-Isidorian Collection. After this period, and when no doubt whatever was any longer entertained of the authenticity of the documents comprised in the Collection, the Popes began to quote them with the same freedom as was used in the case of the Hadrianic Collection. This delay is scarcely consistent with the notion that the forgery owed the success which attended it to the fostering patronage of the Popes. It is in fact a great stretch of credulity to believe that a private Collection of Canons, such as that which goes by the name of Isidore, could have availed to convert the Roman Pontiff from the Bishop of a particular city, country, or collection of Western nations, into the Ecumenical Pastor of the whole Church, the possessor, that is, of singular prerogatives, previously unknown to the Christian world. The marvel is increased when we remember that this change must have come about without any protest being raised, or any remark whatever made, by any of the Bishops, Patriarchs, Provincial and Ecumenical Councils, who were called on to render obedience to a new superior. In truth, it was a time when not only the Latin but also the Greek Church, through its Patriarchs and its Councils, solemnly acknowledged the supreme authority of the Pope. The Patriarch Ignatius, of Constantinople, was no sooner restored to his see, than he gave the most manifest testimony to the divine supremacy of the Roman Pontiff. In his Letter to Nicholas I., he calls the Pope "the Head of us all, and of the Spouse of Christ, the Catholic and Apostolic Church;" and he added that "the words which Christ addressed to St. Peter (St. Matt. xvi. 18, 19) were not confined or limited to the Chief of the Apostles only, but through him were transmitted to all who, after him, should, like him, be Chief Pastors, and most divine sacred Pontiffs of the elder Rome."[1] Nor is this all. Photius himself, on his recal to the Byzantine see, although he had recourse to interpolating the Letters of Pope John VIII., in order to save himself the humiliation of publicly recanting his errors, still did not dare to suppress or alter the plain statement of the Pontifical supremacy, which is evidently contained in the same Papal Letter. Therefore, in the Synod held by him in Constantinople (879), he read to the assembled Bishops the Letter of Pope John to the Emperor Basil, wherein we find the following words: "The Apostolic See received the keys of the Kingdom of Heaven from the Great High Priest Jesus Christ through Peter, the Prince of the Apostles, to whom He said, 'To thee I will give the keys,' &c. By the authority, therefore, of Peter, the Prince of the Apostles, we, in union with the Holy Church, announce to you, and through you to all our holy brothers and fellow-ministers, the Patriarchs of Alexandria, Antioch, and Jerusalem, and all other Bishops and Priests, and to the whole Church of Constantinople, that we consent

[1] *Epist. S. Ignatii Patriarchæ ad Nicholaum Papam* (Labbe, t. x., pp. 517, 518).

and agree to all things which you have asked."[1] And the Pope in this, as well as in other Letters read in the same Synod, went on to inculcate his supreme authority in the Church.[2] When Photius and the other Fathers there assembled were asked by the Papal Legate whether they agreed with those Letters of the Pope, the Patriarch with all the Bishops of the Synod answered, that they perfectly agreed.[3] In the same manner the Oriental Church in the Eighth General Council, held ten years before (869), had given a public testimony to the supreme authority of the Holy See, by unanimously accepting the formulary of union already proposed by Pope Nicholas and sent for acceptance by his successor, Pope Hadrian II. This formulary differed in nothing from the one which Pope Hormisdas obliged the Bishops of the Greek Church to sign at the conclusion of the Acacian schism; it affords one of the clearest testimonies borne by the Universal Church to the divine supreme authority of the Roman Pontiff.[4]

In the second part of his *Christendom's Divisions*, Mr. Ffoulkes passes these over in silence; and yet we were told by a Protestant reviewer that this book was intended to tell the *whole* truth upon the subject discussed. Or does Mr. Ffoulkes believe that the Oriental Church learned the duty of submission to Rome from the compilation of Decretals which had just been put together in France? and that it submitted without

[1] *Epist. Joan. VIII. ad Basilium Imp.*, in Act. ii., Conc. Phot. (Labbe, t. xi., p. 366, seq.).
[2] Labbe, t. xi., pp. 383, 426, seq.
[3] Labbe, l. c., p. 378, et l. c. in n. prec.
[4] In Act. i., Conc. Œcum. viii. (Labbe, t. x., pp. 497, 498, 500).

remark or murmur to this new-forged yoke. Unless he is prepared to admit this paradox, he must join with all the most learned writers of Europe, Protestant no less than Catholic, in confessing that the forgery of the Decretals contributed nothing either to originate and establish, or to propagate the doctrine of Papal supremacy in the Church. The ease with which the False Decretals obtained acceptance and universal recognition as authentic documents, ought itself alone to be sufficient to show that they did not work any change in the groundwork of the constitution of the Church. The genuine Decretals of the successors of Damasus were in the hands of all; these must have been carefully studied by any forger who hoped for success in palming off upon the world a spurious collection of earlier Decretals, and every care would be taken to secure a similarity in language and sentiment between the two series. The forger was therefore obliged, by the conditions of his enterprise, to inculcate no doctrines but such as were currently received in his age, and to choose his materials from sources which were already in credit in the Church. The task of investigating what these sources were, was first undertaken by David Blondel, a Protestant; another Protestant, Kunst, carried on the work, although he added but little to the discoveries of his predecessor; but in our own day the work has been completed by a third Protestant, Hinschius, who, after immense labour and research, has succeeded in tracing up every part and portion of the forged letters to the originals from which they were taken.[1] The conclusion

[1] *Decretales Pseudo-Isidorianæ*, Præf., sec. xv., cap. i., pp. cxi.—cxxxvii.

is that the impostor gathered materials from more than six hundred distinct books in the course of his work; although we need not suppose that he himself used so great a number; for probably he availed himself of summaries and collections already existing before his time.[1]

IV.

But let us now hear Mr. Ffoulkes, who intends to prove by extracts from the Decretals that the prerogatives which they granted to the Pope were unheard of in the Church. "I pass straight," he says, "from these Canons to the Pseudo-Decretals and Pseudo-Donation, that the contrast between them may be seen more readily. For instance, St. Anacletus, in an Encyclic Letter addressed to the Faithful, is made to say: 'Should more difficult questions arise, or should the case be one of high importance, or concern Bishops of high standing, let them be referred, in case of appeal, to the Apostolic See; for this the Apostles appointed by command of our Lord, that all greater and more arduous questions should be brought before the Apostolic See on which Christ founded His Universal Church.'"[2] Mr. Ffoulkes then believes that this forged letter originated a persuasion that the Papal jurisdiction had from time immemorial included within its circle things and persons over which the Popes had in fact never exercised any control, previous to the circulation of the Pseudo-

[1] L. c., pp. cx. et cxxxviii.
[2] *The Church's Creed*, p. 30.

Isidorian Code. In this he is mistaken. First, when once it is proved from Scripture and Tradition that the Popes are the supreme rulers in the Church, their appellate jurisdiction follows as a matter of course, divinely inherent in their office, and independent in its exercise of any regulations formed by Councils. Councils may pass Canons establishing a system of discipline, and regulating the granting of appeals, but they cannot set limits to the power of the Head of the Church, who, when the need arises, can suspend the action of the previous legislation, or supply a new rule to meet fresh emergencies. The genuine Decretals furnish instances in which this power was exercised.[1] But again we deny that the discipline described in the pretended letter of Anacletus was new in the Church at the time of its publication. Long before the appearance of the False Decretals, the Popes had solemnly claimed those rights as part of their divine jurisdiction. Those rights had been already acknowledged by the Canons of Sardica, which were certainly received in the East and in the West alike. In these Canons it had been enacted, not, as Mr. Ffoulkes appears to believe, that only in extreme cases the Bishops were authorised to appeal to the Pope, but, that every Bishop who should think himself to have a fair cause could, after the sentence of the Provincial Synod, appeal to Rome, in order either to obtain a new trial in another province, or to be judged by the Pope himself.[2] Causes then of high importance, and con-

---

[1] We shall return again to this point further on.

[2] "Si aliquis Episcoporum judicatus fuerit in aliqua causa et putat se bonam causam habere ut iterum concilium renovetur; si vobis placet S. Petri Apostoli memoriam honoremus, ut scribatur

cerning Bishops, were, according to the legislation of Sardica, to be referred, in case of appeal, to the See of Rome. Four hundred years before the forgery of the Decretals of Anacletus, Innocent I., writing to Victricius, spoke in accordance with the Canon Law of his age when he said: "If *Causæ Majores* come to be discussed, they are to be referred to the Apostolic See after the judgment of the Bishops; according as the Synod has established, and the holy custom requires."[1] The Pontiff evidently alludes to the Synodic letter which the Council of Sardica addressed to Pope Julius, in which it declared that "It would be an excellent and a most convenient thing that the holy Bishops should refer to the See of the Apostle Peter each, and all, the provinces of the Church."[2] St. Leo I. expressed the same view in several of his Letters. In that addressed to the Metropolitans of Illyricum, he says: "If any appeals or causes of unusual importance occur, our

ab iis qui caussam examinarunt, Julio R. Episcopo, et si judicat renovandum esse judicium, renovetur et det judices," etc. (Can. iii. Conc. Sardic. *Can. Apost. et Conc. Saec.* iv.—vii., selecti a H. T. Bruns, Dr., p. 91. Berolini, 1839). "Cum aliquis Episcopus depositus fuerit eorum episcoporum judicio, qui in vicinis locis commorantur et proclamaverit agendum sibi negotium in urbe Roma; alter Episcopus in ejus cathedra post appellationem ejus qui videtur esse depositus, omnino non ordinetur," etc. (Can. iv., l. c.). "Si Episcopus accusatus fuerit, et judicaverint congregati Episcopi regionis ipsius, et de gradu suo eum dejecerint, si appellaverit qui dejectus est, et confugerit ad Episcopum Rom. Eccl. et voluerit se audiri; si justum putaverit, ut renovetur judicium," etc. (Can. vii.; l. c.). Where are the extreme cases, in which, according to Mr. Ffoulkes, the Bishops were authorised to appeal by the Council of Sardica?

[1] *Epist.* ii. *ad Victricium*, cap. iii., n. 6 (Coustant, p. 749).
[2] *Epist. Syn. Conc. Sardic. ad Julium Papam* (Labbe, t. ii., p. 690).

Decree is that they must be sent to us by the judge; that they may be determined by our sentence according to ecclesiastical usage."[1] The Decree to which the Pope alludes runs as follows: "If a *Causa Major* occur, which our brother there presiding cannot determine, let him send his report to us, and ask our opinion; and we will write in answer whatever the Lord shall suggest to us, to Whom we confess that we owe all our ability; so that ourselves examining the cause, we may assert our right of judgment, in accordance with the long-established discipline and the reverence due to the Apostolic See."[2] The prerogative of the Roman See, which is here claimed by Innocent I. and Leo I., is also assumed, in the most explicit terms, by Gregory I. In a Letter to the Bishop of Arles he says: "If any question concerning faith, or, it may be, on any other subject, arise between Bishops, and is difficult to determine, it must be discussed and settled by an assembly of twelve Bishops. But if no settlement can be arrived at, the question, after argument, must be referred to our tribunal."[3] The same rule is inculcated in other Letters of this Pope to Bishops of the Frankish kingdom;[4] and succeeding Pontiffs agree in enforcing the strict observance of the Canons of Sardica, and of the other laws of the Church which regulate appeals of Bishops. Among others, we may quote Gregory IV.,[5] Leo IV.,[6] and

[1] *Epist.* v. *ad Episcopos per Illyricum*, cap. v. (Op., t. i., p. 619. Edit. Ball.).

[2] In the Epist. vi. of St. Leo to Anastasius Thessal, cap. v. (l. c., p. 622).

[3] *Epist.*, l. v., ep. 53 (Op., t. ii., p. 783. Edit. Maur.).

[4] *Epist.*, l. v., ep. 54 (Op., t. ii., p. 784).

[5] *Epist.* i. *ad Univ. Episc.* (Labbe, t. ix., p. 679).

[6] *Epist.* ii. *ad Episcopos Britanniæ* (Labbe, t. ix., p. 1026).

Benedict III.[1] The civil law itself recognised this part of the ecclesiastical jurisprudence. In the Code of Justinian we read : "We do not allow that anything which concerns the affairs of the Church should pass unreferred to his Blessedness (the Roman Pontiff), for *he is* the Head of all the *holy Priests of God.*"[2] Justinian again, in writing to Pope John II., expresses the same view, calling the Pope *Head of all the Churches.* These words alone might have taught Mr. Ffoulkes that long before the fabrication of the pretended Donation of Constantine, Christian Emperors knew that the Pope was, by divine institution, raised above all Bishops and Patriarchs in the Church. We find proof that the same doctrine was held even among the Nestorian heretics. Ebediesu, in his *Collection of Synodical Canons*, says: "Christ set forth the ministry of the simple Bishops when He breathed on His disciples ; through which inspiration they all and each of them received the power of forgiving and retaining sins. He effectually represented the ministry of the Metropolitans when He stretched His hands over them, and sanctified them by the sign of the Cross, and sent them to preach to the Jews and to the Gentiles alike. Finally, He instituted the Patriarchate which is the Princedom of the Princedoms in the Church, by the giving the keys of the Kingdom of Heaven, which He gave to Simon, when He, the Redeemer of mankind, appointed him Prince of the Apostles, and gave him the presidency over their community by those words—'And thou, being once con-

[1] *Epist.* i. *ad Hincmarum Episc. Rom.* (Labbe, l. c., p. 1249).
[2] *Codex Justinianus,* l. i., tit. i., l. vii. (In *Corp. Juris Civilis cura A. Hermanni*, pt. ii., p. 10. Lipsiæ, 1865).

verted, confirm thy brethren.' Moreover, by entrusting him with the office of feeding His lambs and His sheep, He conferred on him authority over the whole community of the Christians."[1] This is the doctrine which the Popes have ever professed, for they have ever regarded themselves as successors of St. Peter, invested with the same authority as that Apostle for the government of the Church. The documents in proof of this are given in another work, by the present author. It is there shown that the Popes claimed and exercised supreme authority over the Patriarchs of the East, no one of whom ever exercised any such right over a Pope; while Dioscorus of Alexandria, who ventured to attempt something of the kind, was on this account deposed by the Ecumenical Council of Chalcedon.[2] Mr. Ffoulkes takes no notice whatever of all the historical testimonies to this effect which many writers have put together; and he perseveres in his belief that the authority of the Popes over Patriarchs and Bishops owes its origin to the spurious Donation of Constantine. He triumphantly quotes a few lines from that forged document, in which it is said that the Roman See should have dominion as well over the four principal sees of Alexandria, as over all the Churches of God; and he seems to think that he has gained a complete victory. He concludes: "Where have we a syllable of all this in the *genuine* Code of the Church?"[3] We have put the word *genuine* in italics; our readers will

---

[1] Ebediesu, *Collectio Can. Synod. Tr.*, vi., cap. i., transl. ab Assemano (Mai, *Script. Vet. Coll.*, t. x., p. 107, seq.).

[2] Conc. Chalced., Act. v. (Labbe, t. iv., p. 1448).

[3] *The Church's Creed*, p. 31.

understand that allusion is made to the compilation of Justellus, by which our author has been so completely deceived.

V.

With reference to the subject of *Causæ Majores*, or those in which Bishops are concerned, the most approved writers on the Isidorian Decretals, Protestant and Catholic, agree that the object of the writer was to enhance the authority of Bishops, to emancipate them from all control of the civil power, and to secure them shelter and support, in the patronage of the Roman See. Hence, a large portion of the False Decretals bears on the subject of the accusations and trials of Bishops, and on their right of appeal to Rome, the See of their legitimate patron, the Pope. The author insists that causes in which Bishops are concerned, especially when these are of high standing, ought readily to be carried by appeal to Rome; and he does this, not with the object of giving to the successor of St. Peter a jurisdiction which he already possessed and frequently exercised, but in order to encourage these appeals, and thus put some restraint on the violence and injustice of inferior tribunals.[1] The circumstances of the age were such as imperatively required that stress

[1] Hinschius says: "Cum Episcoporum auctoritas illis temporibus accusationibus, dejectionibusque valde diminuta esset, et Benedictus et Pseudo-Isidorus imprimis talibus præcavere multis hac de re statutis, quæ excogitabant, conati sunt" (*Decretales Pseudo-Isidorianæ*, pt. iv., sec. 24, p. ccxxi. Lipsiæ, 1863).

should be laid on the Papal right to receive appeals; in no other way could an efficient stop be put to the growing evils which were destroying the discipline of the Church. At the very time when the False Decretals appeared, a change was going on in the practice of the Church which illustrates what we have said. The forged documents represent the Metropolitans and Primates as judges in the last resort in all causes of the inferior Clergy, who enjoyed no right of appeal to any higher tribunal.[1] Nevertheless, in the middle of the ninth century, appeals of simple Priests to Rome were on the increase. The state of Europe absolutely required this modification in the practical working of the constitution of the Church. But whether such appeals were frequent or not, whether they were provided for and regulated by the Canon Law or were left unnoticed, the prerogative of the Head of the Church remained unaffected; when circumstances called for a modification in discipline, the power to do whatever was needful lay with the Sovereign Pontiff. No law could forbid recourse to the lawful Superior, as often as he saw fit to entertain the case. The instance of Apiarius illustrates this point of Church discipline.[2] But Mr. Ffoulkes denies that the See of Rome was regarded as the ultimate court of appeal, and in proof refers to his favourite Code of the Universal Church. Setting Justellus aside for a moment, we will give a few extracts from Letters of early Popes, which show that

[1] *Epist.* i. *Eleutherii*, cap. ii. (*Decretales Isidorianæ*, p. 125. Editæ ab Hinschio.)
[2] See what is written on this subject in the *Papal Supremacy*, sec. v., n. v., p. 149.

the Popes owe their jurisdiction not to Isidore but to
Christ our Lord, and that their right to receive appeals
was acknowledged and exercised many centuries before
the famous forgery was concocted. Thus Pope Zosimus,
writing to the Fathers of the Council of Carthage, uses
the following expressions:[1] "Although the tradition of
the Fathers has assigned so great an authority to the
Apostolic See, that no one *should dare to dispute about
a judgment* given by it,[2] and that See, by various causes
and regulations, has maintained this right; and the
discipline of the Church, in the laws which it follows,
still pays due reverence to the name of Peter, from
whom that See descends, for Canonical antiquity, by
universal consent, willed that so great a power should
belong to that Apostle—a power also derived from the
actual promise of Christ our God—that it should be his
to loose what was bound, and to bind what was loosed,
an equal state of power being bestowed upon those
who by God's will should be found worthy to inherit
his See, for he has charge both of all the Churches and
especially of this wherein he sate; nor does he allow
any storm to shake any portion of the privilege, or any
part of the sentence of that See to which he has given
his name as a foundation, firm and not to be weakened
by any violence whatever—of that See which no one
can rashly attack but at his own peril. Although, then,
Peter is of so great authority (as has been confirmed by
subsequent Decrees of the Fathers), that by all laws and
regulations, both human and divine, the Roman Church
is strengthened; and although you are not ignorant that

[1] *Epist.* xii., n. 1 (Coustant, p. 974).
[2] "Ut de ejus judicio disceptare nullus auderet" (*Ibid.*).

we rule over his place, and are in possession also of the authority of his name, nevertheless, though *so great be our authority that no one may reconsider our sentence,*" &c.[1] Now, if the Pope judges with such an authority that no one is allowed to dispute about his judgments, that no portion of them can be shaken, that no one may reject or reconsider his decisions—and if, at the same time, his authority is that of St. Peter, and rests on Christ's promises, we must conclude that the Pope was divinely appointed to be supreme judge, without any control or appeal whatever in the Church. Boniface I., in his Letter to the Bishops of Macedonia, Achaia, &c., expressed the same view.[2] "No one," he says, "ever attempted to lift up his hand against the Apostolic greatness, *from whose judgment there is no appeal whatever.*[3] No one ever dared to rebel against it, except he who wished to pronounce a sentence of damnation against himself." These words evidently imply the doctrine that the Roman See was the ultimate court of appeal. Again, Pope Boniface, in the same Letter, refers to Peter as the source of the authority of the Roman See, and consequently claims a divine origin for the constitution by which that See is the ultimate court of appeal in the Church. Pope Gelasius spoke with even greater explicitness. "The See of the blessed Peter," he declares, "has the right of rescinding the sentence of any Bishop whatever, since it has the right of judging the whole Church; but no one has any right to appeal

---

[1] "Cum tantum nobis esset auctoritatis, ut nullus de nostra possit retractare sententia" (Coustant, p. 975).

[2] Bonifacius I., *Epist.* xv., n. 5 (Coustant, p. 1042).

[3] "De cujus judicio non licet retractari" (l. c.).

from its judgments, for the Canons allow any one from any part of the world to appeal to Rome, but they forbid all appeal from the decisions of Rome."[1] These few extracts are clear enough, and dispense us from the necessity of producing any more quotations. Gelasius agrees with all his predecessors in stating that the Roman See has the supreme power in the Church and is the ultimate court of appeal, since it has the right to judge all the Bishops of the whole Church, and to receive appeals from all the ecclesiastical tribunals of the world, but its decisions are without control and not subject to any appeal whatsoever. Its decisions bind all the Church, and any resistance to them would make the impugner an outcast from the pale of Christ. In a word, all and each in the Church must submit to the sentence of the Roman Pontiff— *Ut capiti membra concordent*, "That the members may be in agreement with the Head," as St. Leo spoke in his Letter to Theodoret, Bishop of Cyr.[2]

[1] *Epist.* xiii. *ad Episcopos Dardaniæ* (Labbe, t. v., p. 328).
[2] *Epist.* cxx. *ad Theodoretum Episc. Cyri.* (Op., t. i., p. 1219).

VI.

Mr. Ffoulkes expresses surprise at not seeing, in the famous *Code of the Universal Church*, " any mention whatever of the See of Rome as a supreme power, or even ultimate court of appeal."[1] We answer that the object of Decrees of Councils is twofold—dogma and discipline. When a Council is dealing with questions of dogma it does not legislate, but it defines that some particular doctrine is revealed, or that it must be understood in one and not in another sense ; and, at the same time, the Bishops condemn all who do not accept the doctrine and its explanation from their mouth. But it is not usual for Councils to deal in any way with revealed doctrine, except when forced to do so by heretics or infidels who attack and deny the truth, or who misrepresent it. As to matters of discipline, it is the province of Councils to enact Canons for the interior regulation of the Church ; but they have no power to alter the Church's essential constitution as established by Christ, and therefore they cannot touch the jurisdiction which by divine right is the necessary prerogative of the Head of the Church. With the sanction of the Supreme Pastor they can make laws to regulate the ordinary exercise of his jurisdiction, but they cannot limit the jurisdiction itself, so that the Pontiff will always be left at liberty to act, when he sees fit, *ex plenitudine potestatis*—" in the fulness of his authority," uncontrolled by any Synod whatever. Now, during the first nine centuries no heretic arose to make a direct

[1] *The Church's Creed*, p. 28.

attack upon the doctrine of Papal supremacy, and therefore no mention of the doctrine is found in the decrees of faith of the first seven General Councils; still less could any reference to it be expected in the Code of Justellus, which does not comprise matter of later date than the middle of the fifth century. The argument drawn by Mr. Ffoulkes from the silence of this Code would equally avail to disprove the doctrine of the Seven Sacraments, or of the Real Presence in the Eucharist; and, in fact, this argument is sometimes found in the works of Protestant controversialists. But the answer is easy. The Seven Sacraments were never denied in the Church before the time of the Reformation, and therefore the faith regarding them was first defined by the Council of Trent. Wiclyffe was the first who persistently, and with the sympathy of a large number of followers, denied the Real Presence, and therefore no definition of it can be found before the Council of Constance, when the errors of that heretic were anathematised. In like manner, the Photian schism was the earliest period at which any mention will be found of the Papal supremacy in the way of definition, for it had never been directly attacked before that time. But in the Eighth General Council (869), the Greek Bishops and Patriarchs signed the formula of Hormisdas, which, by virtue of the adhesion of the East as well as the West, became an unimpeachable definition of faith; and in this formula the supremacy of the Roman See is stated in the strongest terms.[1] The Greek schism, nevertheless, continued, and developed

[1] See it in Denzinger's *Enchiridion Symb. et Definit.*, n. xx., p. 49. Edit. 1865.

itself into heresy against the doctrine of the Papal authority, and this doctrine was therefore defined again and again, as of faith, A.D. 1215, in the Fourth Lateran Council;[1] again, A.D. 1274, in the Second of Lyons;[2] and again, A.D. 1439, in the Council of Florence.[3] A very ordinary acquaintance with theological principles would have taught Mr. Ffoulkes that when a General Council defines that a doctrine is of faith, it at the same time teaches that this doctrine was a part of the deposit once received by the Apostles, and imparted by them to the Church, to be handed down in the uninterrupted succession of Pastors. This being so, there is no ground for surprise if a doctrine, taught clearly by one Synod, has been passed over in silence by preceding General Councils. The Church is indefectible in existence and in doctrine; it is, then, always the same, and cannot contradict itself. The infallibility of the Universal Church was admitted in principle by Calvin himself. Does Mr. Ffoulkes dispute it?

But we have a further answer to this difficulty. The Acts and Decrees of the Councils of the first four centuries continually, by necessary implication, teach the doctrine of Papal supremacy. A careful search into the Acts of the Councils of Ephesus and Chalcedon suffices to show that the doctrine of the supreme authority of the Pope was at that time firmly established in the persuasion and in the practice of the Church.

---

[1] *De Privilegiis Sedium Patriarchalium*, cap. v. (In Denzinger, n. lii., p. 157).

[2] *Confessio Fidei Michaelis Palæologi oblata in Conc. Lugd.* ii. *Gregorio X.* (In Denzinger, l. c., n. lix., p. 170).

[3] *Decretum Unionis Conc. Florentini* (In Denzinger, l. c., n. lxxiii., p. 201).

But there is no need here to draw out at length the proofs which are collected elsewhere;[1] it will be sufficient to call attention to the clear argument furnished by the well-known Third, Fourth, and Seventh Canons of Sardica. When the Council of Sardica passed Canons regulating the practice of appeals in the causes of Bishops, it did not confer any new jurisdiction upon the Pope. The Fourth Canon evidently presupposes such an appellate jurisdiction; it ordains that, in case of appeal by a Bishop to Rome from a provincial sentence of deposition, the vacant see should not be filled up pending the hearing of the appeal. The Seventh Canon is to the same effect. The Synod of Sardica, then, solemnly acknowledged the supreme authority of the Roman Pontiff in receiving appeals from the Universal Church; it did not constitute any new rights nor grant a new privilege to the See of Rome. The history of the first four centuries of the Church, no less than that of the following ages, evidently proves the existence of a practice whereby the Pope received appeals of Bishops from all parts of the world. Cardinal Pitra adduces in proof of this the testimony of three writers who, as being Orientals and schismatics, are most unexceptionable witnesses—Aristenus, Zonaras, and Balsamon.[2] So conscious were some of the older Eastern schismatics of the force of the argument drawn from the Canons of Sardica, that they endeavoured to show that this Council had not been received in the Greek Church,

---

[1] *Supreme Authority of the Pope*, sec. iv., n. iii., seq., p. 84, seq.
[2] *Juris Eccl. Græcorum, Hist. et Mon.*, t. i. Romæ, 1864. *Conc. Sardic. Annot.*, p. 485.

but they were unable to prove their historical paradox.[1] Balsamon and others adopted a contrary view, saying that the Patriarch of Constantinople, like a second Pope, enjoyed the same privilege of receiving appeals.[2] Mr. Ffoulkes adopts the same course. "Against them" (the Canons of Sardica), he says, "we must always remember is to be set the Ninth Canon of the Fourth Council—'If any Bishop,' &c. More persons are thus authorised to appeal to the see of Constantinople than in the Sardican Canons themselves to Rome."[3] There is, however, no ground for thus setting up the Ninth Canon of Chalcedon in rivalry with the Canons of Sardica, which harmonise perfectly both with the Ninth and the Seventeenth Canons of the Fourth General Council. The Canons of Chalcedon regulate the procedure in ecclesiastical causes in the first or second instance, within a single province or portion of the Church; at Sardica, the legislation concerned the whole Church and regulated appeals to the highest tribunal. In fact, the Ninth and Seventeenth Canons of Chalcedon cannot, properly speaking, be said to deal in any way with appeals; their object really is to establish a new tribunal of the first instance, with jurisdiction to dispose of causes which might arise between Metropolitans on the one hand, and their Suffragan Bishops, or any of their Clergy, on the other. The first part of the Ninth Canon is occupied with an enumeration of the tribunals proper to each class of ecclesiastical causes;

[1] *Conc. Sardic. Annot.*, p. 484, seq.
[2] Balsamon, *Canones Conc. Sardic.*, pp. 856, 859; in Can. xii. Synodi Antioch., p. 821, seq. Lut. Paris., 1620.
[3] *The Church's Creed*, p. 29.

in the second part, the Fathers merely go on to make an exception for the case in which the Metropolitan himself is engaged in some question with one of his Bishops or of his Clergy. "If any Bishop or Clerk," they say, "should have a dispute with his Metropolitan, he may apply to the Exarch of his diocese, or else to the throne of Constantinople, and have the case tried here." That appeals could be made from the Bishop's tribunal to that of the Metropolitan, and from this to the Patriarch, has never been denied, nor can it be denied by any one who is acquainted with the One Hundred and Eleventh Canon of the Council of Carthage.[1] But the Canons did not allow any cause to be treated in first instance by the Exarch or Patriarch, except in the two cases pointed out by the Ninth and Seventeenth Canons of Chalcedon, in which a legal prejudice was created which disabled the Metropolitan from exercising the functions of a judge. The same view is taken by Balsamon.[2]

But we must go on to consider whether it is true that the Ninth and Seventeenth Canons of Chalcedon gave to the Patriarch of Constantinople the privilege of judging causes of Bishops and Metropolitans of the other Patriarchates of the East.[3] (1.) It is certain that

---

[1] Conc. Carthag. iii., Can. x. "Ut a quibuscumque judicibus ecclesiasticis ad alios judices ecclesiasticos ubi est major auctoritas provocare liceat" (Labbe, t. ii., p. 1401).

[2] Op. cit., in Syn. Chalced., Can. ix., p. 334.

[3] Some instances of jurisdictional power exercised by the Patriarch of Constantinople beyond the boundaries of their ordinary jurisdiction, are fully explained by the learned Lupus, *Scholia et Notæ in Conc. Chalced., Can.* ix. (Op., t. ii., p. 79. Venetiis, 1724).

no one of the Byzantine Patriarchs ever claimed this privilege, although ambition might well have led them to aspire to it. (2.) It is also certain that Justinian, who was so anxious to exalt the power of his imperial city, decreed that, according to the ecclesiastical laws, Metropolitans should be treated only before their own Patriarch.[1] We find the same law inserted in the *Basilica* ;[2] and it is inserted by the grasping Photius himself in his *Nomocanon*.[3] (3.) It is likewise certain that the Greek Canonists, as Balsamon, Zonaras, Blastares, &c., maintain the same Canonical principle— that it is not allowed to carry a cause from one Patriarchate to another, either in the first instance, or by way of appeal to another Patriarch.[4] (4.) The Canons mentioned above must be considered in connection with the famous Twenty-eighth Canon of the same Council of Chalcedon. Now in that Canon, the Patriarch of Constantinople sought to obtain a legal sanction for the Patriarchal prerogatives claimed by his see over the dioceses of Asia and Pontus and the Church of Thrace. That is to say, he sought to obtain the jurisdiction of ordaining those three Metropolitans. But the jurisdiction of ordaining cannot be detached from that of judging; he asked, therefore, that judicial authority should be

---

[1] *Nov.* cxxiii., cap. xxii. (*Juris Civilis*, t. iii., p. 554. Lipsiæ, 1865). See also *Nov.* cxxxvii., cap. v. (l. c., p. 627).

[2] *Basilicorum*, l. iii., tit. i., leg. xxxviii. et xxxix., t. i., pp. 104, 105. Edit. G. E. Heimbach. Lipsiæ, 1833.

[3] *Nomocanon*, tit. ix., cap. i. (Op., t. iv., p. 1098, seq. Edit. Migne), et tit. ix., cap. vi., p. 1102 ; *Syntagma Canonum*, tit. ix., cap. v. (l. c., p. 727).

[4] Balsamon, Op. cit., in *Syn. Antioch. Sch. in Can.* xi., p. 819, seq.

granted him in those Metropolitan Churches. It follows then that the Ninth Canon concerning the Bishop of Constantinople cannot have gone beyond those limits; otherwise we should have the strange result that in the Ninth Canon the very Council should grant to the Byzantine Patriarch so extensive a jurisdiction all over the East, which in the Twenty-eighth limited this jurisdiction to his Metropolitan dioceses. Photius himself, explaining the imperial constitutions concerning the boundaries of the Constantinopolitan Patriarchate, maintains no more than that the Bishop of Constantinople has jurisdiction.[1] We must then conclude that Mr. Ffoulkes has quoted a Canon which has nothing to do with the controversy in hand, and, moreover, which does not impart to the Patriarch of Constantinople any privilege which was not enjoyed by the other Patriarchs in the East over their own Metropolitans. But as to the jurisdiction of the Roman Pontiff which is implied in the Canons of Sardica, the case is wholly different. Balsamon himself is forced to acknowledge this, and in doing so betrays great embarrassment while attempting to reconcile the prerogatives of the Roman Pontiff with the authority claimed on behalf of the see of Constantinople.[2] Let us compare the practice of appeals, according to the discipline which flourished in the East, with the jurisdiction of the Roman See as recognised by the Council of Sardica, and constantly exercised by the Popes. The law on appeals in the East may be summed up under the following heads: First, the Patriarchs cannot receive appeals in cases arising

[1] *Nomocanon*, tit. i., cap. vi. (l. c., p. 989, seq.).
[2] Balsamon, Op. cit., l. c., p. 821.

beyond the limits of their Patriarchate ; secondly, they have no jurisdiction over other Patriarchs ; thirdly, from their judgment there is no appeal.[1] Now, first, the Roman Pontiff received appeals not only from his own Patriarchate, but also from all parts of the Church, and instances of the exercise of this right abound in history ; secondly, he exercised full jurisdiction, as we remarked above, over all the Eastern Patriarchs, and judged, condemned, and deposed them with an authority subject to no control ; thirdly, he received appeals from sentences of the Patriarchs themselves, of which history furnishes many examples. We must then conclude that the jurisdiction of the Pope is higher than that of any Patriarch, since it is exercised over them also, and includes the right to judge, condemn, and depose them without any appeal whatever. The Roman Pontiff may well be called the Prince of all Patriarchs, because he is the successor of the Prince of the Apostles, whose privileges he inherits for the government of the Church.

We may here call attention to another point on which Mr. Ffoulkes betrays ignorance of the principles which from the earliest times regulated the legislation of the Church. He is manifestly unaware that the same weight was always ascribed to Papal Decretals as to the Canons of Councils. All the ancient Collections of Canons—we may mention in particular those of Dionysius Exiguus, and of Hadrian—carefully gathered together the Decretals of the Roman Pontiffs as a most important source of law, of authority no way inferior to that of the General Councils. In the same spirit we saw

[1] Photius admits this general principle in his *Nomocanon*, tit. ix., cap. vi., and in his *Syntagma Can.*, tit. ix., cap. vi., pp. cit.

Leo IV. and Nicholas I. placing the Decrees of their
predecessors in an equal rank with the Canons of Nicæa
themselves. Nor was this any new doctrine in the ninth
century; it was perfectly familiar four hundred years
before the time of Nicholas. Siricius, a Pope of the
fourth century, in his Letter to Himmerius, declares that
all the Bishops are bound to know the venerable Decrees
enacted either by the Apostolic See or by the Synodical
Canons.[1] Innocent I. and Celestine I. taught the same,[2]
and in the same spirit Pope Gelasius ordered that the
Decretals of the Roman Pontiffs should be received with
great veneration;[3] while Pope Leo the Great solemnly
declared that the Decrees of all his predecessors were to
be observed in such a manner that their violation should
not escape punishment.[4] Consistently with this doctrine,
the Popes were always accustomed to allege the laws of
their own predecessors and the Canons of Councils as
possessing the same weight of authority. There is no
need to adduce a long series of quotations in proof of
this assertion; they may be found in abundance in the

---

[1] Siricius, *Epist.* i., n. 20 (Coustant, p. 637). "Statuta Sedis
Apostolicæ vel Canonum venerabilia definita nulli Sacerdotum
Domini ignorare sit licitum."

[2] Innoc. I., *Epist.* ii., n. 2 (Coustant, p. 748); Cœlest. I.,
Epist. v., n. 1 (Coustant, p. 1072).

[3] "Decretales epistolas quas beatissimi Papæ diversis temporibus ab urbe Roma pro diversorum Patrum consultatione dederunt,
venerabiliter suscipiendas esse" (*Decretum Gelasii*, in Conc. Rom. i.,
n. iv. Labbe, t. v., p. 387).

[4] "Omnia Decretalia Constituta tam beatæ memoriæ Innocentii, quam omnium decessorum nostrorum, quæ de ecclesiasticis
ordinibus et canonum promulgata sunt disciplinis, ita a vestra
dilectione custodiri debere mandamus, ut si quis in illa commiserit,
veniam sibi deinceps noverit denegari" (*Epist.* iv., cap. v. Op.,
t. i., p. 616. Edit. Baller.).

Epistles of the Popes, from the time when Innocent I. appealed to the Letter of Siricius,[1] down to the days of Nicholas the Great, who cites Julius,[2] Celestine,[3] Innocent,[4] Gelasius,[5] Leo,[6] and others, in terms not distinguishable from those in which he employs the Canons of the early Synods. This practice alone supplies evident proofs of the supreme authority of the Popes over the whole Church. No jurisdiction short of this would have authorised them in treating their decisions as universal laws binding upon all Christians; and since we have seen the practice in use long before the middle of the ninth century, when the False Decretals appeared, it is clear that the world-wide authority of which we speak is not to be attributed to the influence of that famous forgery. So far we have been dealing with the question how far the False Decretals can be considered as having influenced the doctrine of the Church; we now proceed to the discussion whether any changes of discipline can be traced to the same source.

[1] *Epist.* vi. *ad Exuperium*, n. 2 (Coustant, p. 790).
[2] In *Epist.* viii. (Labbe, t. ix., p. 1340).
[3] *Ibid.*, l. c., p. 1323.
[4] In *Epist.* lxx. (Labbe, l. c., p. 1491), et in *Epist.* iv., in App. (Labbe, l. c., p. 1506).
[5] In *Epist.* ix. (Labbe, l. c., p. 1353).
[6] *Ibid.*, l. c., p. 1350.

VII.

Mr. Ffoulkes asserts confidently that the forgery was used as an instrument for introducing so great innovations, that he represents the whole system of government in the Church as having undergone a complete change in the middle of the ninth century. In proof of this position, our author refers to an article on the False Decretals, from the pen of Père Régnon, which appeared in the *Etudes*,[1] and he then continues, as though the words he has quoted were conclusive of the whole question, "Have I said more than this— namely, that our existing system originated with, and is based on, the Pseudo-Decretals?"[2] These words necessarily lead the reader to believe that in the opinion of Père Régnon the False Decretals gave rise to a new system of doctrine and discipline in the Church, exactly as is maintained by Mr. Ffoulkes. It is difficult to see what could have occasioned so strange a misapprehension of the meaning of the French Jesuit, whose words are perfectly clear. He merely follows in the steps of Hinschius: " Puis donc que le jugement des évêques mis au rang des causes majeures a été la pierre de touche pour reconnaître quand et comment le Pape Nicolas I. a connu et cité les Fausses Décrétales; puisque soixante dix Fausses Décrétales sur quatre-vingts ne traitent pas un autre sujet ; puisque de l'aveu de tous, ce point est le seul qui ait excité des réclamations au IX. siècle, n'est-il-pas naturel de conclure que

---

[1] *Etudes Rélig. Hist. et Litt.*, t. x., Nouv. Série, p. 382, seq.
[2] *The Church's Creed*, p. 38.

c'est là précisément ce qui résume toute la réforme pseudo-isidorienne."[1] Père Régnon then goes on to say, "Cette nouvelle discipline était bonne assurément. Adoptée par Saint Nicolas le Grand, en 865 ; par le huitième Concile Œcuménique en 870, confirmée par le Concile de Trente en 1564, elle est depuis neuf siècles le droit commun dans l'Eglise Catholique," &c.[2] These last words alone are produced by Mr. Ffoulkes, and being detached from the preceding they are made to convey a meaning which was never contemplated by the writer. It is clear that Père Régnon confines the change of discipline to the "jugement des évêques mis au rang des causes majeures." That is to say, the sentence of a Metropolitan, or of the Provincial Synod, against a Bishop, was not to be definitive without the previous sanction of the Pope. That this and no other was the mind of Père Régnon is evident—(1.) from his own words which precede the extract quoted by Mr. Ffoulkes ; (2.) from his quotation of the Letter of Nicholas, of the Twenty-sixth Canon of the Eighth Ecumenical Synod, and of the Council of Trent, Sess. xxiv., cap. 5, *De Reformatione;*[3] (3.) it is also manifest from the first article on the same subject written by the same writer, and inserted in another volume of the *Etudes*.[4] In this place Père Régnon declares what we have all along maintained : " La manière dont les Fausses Décrétales ont été introduites et acceptées est, à elle seule, une preuve péremptoire qu'elles n'opéraient point dans la

---

[1] *Etudes* cit., l. c., p. 391, seq.
[2] *Ibid.*, p. 392. Quoted by Mr. Ffoulkes in p. 37, seq.
[3] We will return to this subject further on.
[4] *Etudes*, t. v., p. 477, seq.

discipline ecclésiastique une révolution telle que l'attribution au Pontife Romain d'une primauté ou des droits dont on n'aurait pas eu l'idée." He then produces the authority of the learned brothers Ballerini, who speak to the same effect, and then goes on: "Que le IX. siècle ait pris pour l'ancienne discipline une discipline dont on n'avait jamais entendu parler avant le Pseudo-Isidore; qu'il ait accepté de confiance des documents ou il apprenait (ce qu'il avait ignoré jusque-là) que les évêques de Rome avaient juridiction sur tous les autres évêques, qu'ils avaient le droit de réserver les causes majeures, de recevoir tous les appels, et de juger toutes les causes en dernier ressort; *voila ce qu'on ne persuadera jamais à des hommes sérieux.*" And in the same place he reduces the reforms introduced by the Pseudo-Decretals to "des modifications de détail," and "à tirer quelques nouvelles conséquences pratiques des principes universellement admis."[1] In the other article, which will be found in the tenth volume of the *Etudes*, he specifies these modifications of detail, and the practical consequences derived from principles already admitted, and he sums them up in the one rule that causes of Bishops were to be referred to Rome for a definitive sentence.

Mr. Ffoulkes certainly does not agree with these views of Father Régnon, whom he has himself chosen to cite as an authority. We are content with his choice, and call on him to bow to the decision of the judge whom he has himself selected. For our own part, we admit the view put forward by Father Régnon, and by Hinschius, whom he follows, only under the form given

[1] *Etudes*, t. v., p. 478.

in the article inserted in the fifth volume of the *Etudes*, to which a note in the tenth volume evidently refers.[1] In other words, we regard the change introduced into the discipline of the Church through the influence of the False Decretals, as affecting points of detail only, or rather as being no more than the practical application of principles already universally admitted. Hinschius believes that the change was greater, and he supports his view principally by reference to passages in the Letters ascribed to Eleutherius,[2] Victor,[3] Zephyrinus,[4] and Xistus II.[5] The passage of St. Eleutherius runs as follows : " Definitive sentences against Bishops are to be brought to this Holy See alone, and to be confirmed by its authority, as was decreed by the Apostles with the consent of many Bishops." And St. Victor adds: " Although the Bishops of the province are at liberty to look into the cause of any accused Bishop, yet they must not pass sentence without consulting the Roman Pontiff, for it is to St. Peter and no other that the words were addressed — 'Whatsoever thou shalt bind on earth,' &c." The others express exactly the same view, and are made to use nearly the same words. Now we maintain that these Decretals contain nothing but the practical application of a principle of law which was already known and admitted in the Church. Let us compare the language used by Pope Julius in addressing the Eusebians, who had ventured to pro-

[1] *Etudes*, t. x., p. 397.
[2] *Epist. Eleutherii*, cap. ii. (*Decretales Pseudo-Isidorianæ*, p. 125. Edit. ab Hinschio).
[3] *Epist.* i. *Victoris*, cap. v. (*Decret.* cit., p. 128).
[4] *Epist.* i. *S. Zephyrini*, cap. vi. (*Decret.* cit., p. 132).
[5] *Epist. Xisti II.*, cap. ii. (*Decret.* cit., p. 190).

nounce a Synodical sentence against St. Athanasius: "If," he says, "they (the Bishops condemned) had any fault, the judgment ought to be pronounced according to the Ecclesiastical Canons. It was then necessary to write to us, that a just decision might be given by all. Because they who suffered were Bishops, and the Churches which were afflicted were those noble Churches which the Apostles governed by themselves. Why, then, was nothing reported to us concerning the Alexandrine Church? Are you not aware that this is the custom, to write first to us, that from hence may be determined what is just? If some suspicion had arisen against the Bishop of that town it was necessary to write to this Church."[1] Socrates and Sozomen alluded to this Letter of Julius to the Eusebians, and especially to the above passage, when they said that there is a Sacerdotal Canon which declares everything null and void which is enacted without the sanction of the Bishop of Rome.[2] The two Greek historians knew well what was the Canonical principle ruling the Church with regard to trials of Bishops, and therefore, far from blaming Pope Julius' claims, they justified them, and declared them to be in accordance with the Canons. Pope Innocent I. expressed the same idea in yet more general and comprehensive terms. "No cause," he says, "is to be regarded by the Fathers as settled until it has been submitted to this See, however remote the province in which it may have arisen;"[3] and he maintains that

---

[1] *Epist.* i. *Julii Papæ ad Eusebianos*, n. 22 (Coustant, p. 386, seq.).
[2] Socrates, *Hist. Eccl.*, l. ii., cap. xvii. (Edit. Valesius, p. 94); Sozomenus, *Hist. Eccl.*, l. iii., cap. x. (Edit. Valesii, p. 510).
[3] *Epist.* xxix. *ad Conc. Carthagin*, n. i. (Coustant, p. 889).

this is the rule established "in the Church by the Apostles themselves, and in particular by St. Peter, from whom flows the authority of the Roman See."

To these extracts others could be added taken from the Letters of succeeding Popes; but what we have laid before our readers should be sufficient to prove that the maxim concerning the episcopal causes as requiring the sentence of the Roman See, had found place in the law of the Church long before the time of the Pseudo-Decretals. That maxim, it is true, was not generally enforced in practice, and the reason is obvious: if a Bishop condemned by the Provincial Synod had felt aggrieved it was in his power to appeal to Rome, but if he acquiesced in the sentence, and declined to appeal, in ordinary circumstances that would have been a proof of his guilt and of the justice of his condemnation. In such a case, then, the interference of Rome could have no place, for crime has no claim to protection. But as soon as the deplorable state of society rendered necessary the practical application of that Canonical principle, the Pseudo-Isidore insisted upon it, with the purpose of sheltering the Bishops from violence, and of protecting their authority and their power. In fact, the False Decretals have never exercised any influence in the East.[1] Nevertheless, in the Eighth General Council, the assembled Fathers appointed the Patriarchal See as the tribunal in first instance of Bishops accused of

---

[1] On this point we disagree with Father Régnon, who looks upon the Twenty-sixth Canon of the Fourth Synod of Constantinople as having been enacted in consequence of the False Decretals.

any crime.¹ They acted thus in order to do away with the imperial delegations concerning the causes of the Bishops, from which so many evils had arisen in the Church.² The fact of the Bishops being placed under the immediate jurisdiction of the Patriarchs was an implicit declaration that the episcopal causes were to be regarded as *Causæ Majores*. Consequently, the Decree of the Eighth Council turned into a regular law of the Church the principle inculcated by Julius in the cause of St. Athanasius, and which Innocent I. subsequently pointed out to the Synod of Carthage. If then, the Popes, subsequently to the ninth century, considered episcopal causes as *Causæ Majores*, and accordingly ordered that they should be determined at Rome, they did not act upon the authority of the Decretals, but upon a maxim of ecclesiastical jurisprudence which was enforced by their predecessors, and which the course of circumstances had caused to be universally received as a necessary part of ecclesiastical discipline. Nicholas I. furnishes us another proof in one of his Letters to Hincmar, as well as his well-known Address to the Bishops of France on the cause of Rothade, Bishop of Soisson. In these he speaks almost in the very words of Pope Julius and Pope Innocent I.,³ and refers to their authority no less than to that of Leo's Letter to Anastasius of Thessalonica.⁴ Moreover, he proves from

---

[1] Conc. Constantinop. iv., Act. x., Can xxvi. (Labbe, t. x., p. 649).
[2] See Lupus, in Synod viii., Can. xxvi. (Op., t. iii., p. 314).
[3] See *Epist.* xxviii. *Nicolai Papæ ad Hincmarum* (Labbe, t. x., p. 1425), and *Epist. ejusdem ad Univ. Episcopos Galliæ* (Labbe, t. x., pp. 281, 282).
[4] *Epist.* lxxiv., p. 683. Edit. Ball.

the character and office of the Bishops that their causes are to be considered as *Causæ Majores*. But he does not mention any of the Pseudo-Decretals in order to prove his assertion; nor did he need to do so.

VIII.

But the defenders of Papal authority, and even Popes themselves, have made frequent appeals to the Pseudo-Decretals in support of the prerogatives of the Roman See! This is the great objection on which Mr. Ffoulkes expatiates with an air of triumph. He tells us that the Pseudo-Decretals were employed against the Greeks in the Florentine Council; and by Leo IX. in his Letter to Cerularius; that Eugenius IV. used them in his Instructions to the Armenians; that the Catechism of the Council of Trent refers to them when treating both of the Papal authority and of the Sacrament of Confirmation;[1] finally, that although the Popes had it in their power to ascertain the genuine or spurious character of the documents, yet they studiously forbore from inquiry, and said nothing.[2] Let us shortly examine these various assertions. First, is it true that the Popes of the ninth and the following centuries were able to ascertain whether the Pseudo-Isidorian Decretals were or were not genuine missives of their predecessors in the earliest centuries? Certainly not. It is well known that the greater part of the Letters of the early

[1] *The Church's Creed*, pp. 31—33.
[2] *Ibid.*, p. 27.

Popes, during the first centuries of persecution, were lost. Nicholas himself says of the Decretals of his predecessors, especially of the first age of the Church, that only some (*nonnulla*) of their writings still existed in the Archives.¹ This is in direct contradiction to the assertion of Mr. Ffoulkes that the Popes "must have known from the first, or been able to ascertain, whether they came from their Archives or not."² How could they know this when the Letters of the earliest Popes did not exist in their Archives? It is true that criticism might well have excited suspicion as to the genuineness of the Isidorian Collection. But in an uncritical age criticism had no power and no real existence. The age was unable, as Mr. Palmer says, to distinguish the marks of the forgeries.³ The Decretals which "purported to embody the formal teaching of the earliest of the Popes" did not imply any doctrine, or any part of ecclesiastical discipline, which was contrary either to the dogma or the ruling maxims of the Church. The power ascribed to the Roman Pontiffs in these Letters was that which they had always possessed and exercised; the episcopal office, far from being depressed, was rather strengthened and sheltered against all attacks whatever of outward violence.⁴ There was then nothing

¹ *Epist.* vii., cit. (l. c., p. 282). See on this subject Fr. Ryder's *Critique upon Mr. Ffoulkes' Letter*, n. ii., p. 32, seq.
² *The Church's Creed*, p. 27.
³ *The Church of Christ*, pt. vii., ch. viii., vol. ii., p. 431. Third edition.
⁴ We have already quoted Hinschius in support of this view. The view is now generally received by all the most learned men who have occupied themselves with critical researches upon this Collection. See Walter (*Droit Ecclés.*, sec. 92, p. iii. Paris, 1840); Phillips (*Droit Ecclés. dans ses sources*, trad. par Crouzet, ch. i.,

which we could expect to awaken the suspicion of the Supreme Rulers of the Church. That "it was enough for the Popes that their genuineness came to be generally believed in, that they favoured her aggrandisement, and could be employed with decisive effect against those who contested it," is a mere calumny to which Mr. Ffoulkes has given fresh currency, and which we have already refuted.

But in truth the Popes acted in this matter with very great prudence and reserve. We have already mentioned that the whole Collection of the Pseudo-Decretals was not universally known and received in Rome before the middle of the eleventh century; before the time of Leo IX., only Hadrian II. and Stephen V. had alleged them in their Letters. Other Pontiffs made no account of them whatever. Nay, in the Synod of Gersteingen (1085), Otto, Cardinal and Pontifical Legate (who was afterwards Pope Urban II.) spoke of them with contempt.[1] But after a time the Popes found that the whole Collection was universally received as authoritative by the most learned men of the age, and admitted in all private compilations of Canon Law; and no reason could be assigned to justify any further hesitation on the part of Rome. And here we must repeat what we have so often said: that no part of the doctrine or discipline of the Church in any manner rested upon the False Decretals. The same dogmas and the same discipline

sec. 9, p. 58); Denzinger (*Ecloge et Epicrisis*, cit. In Migne, *PP. LL.*, t. cxxx., p. xi.); Hefele (In the *Dictionnaire Théologique*, trad. par J. Goschler, *Act. Pseudo-Isidore*, t. xix., p. 368, seq.), &c.

[1] See Phillips, l. c., n. 43, p. 59; Denzinger, l. c., p. xiv.

had existed for eight centuries before the age of the Pseudo-Isidore, and they continued to exist without change when the Decretals were spread all over the Church, and were received on every side as authentic documents. It follows that neither doctrine nor discipline were in any way prejudiced if appeal was made to the Forged Letters, either by private theologians or by the Popes themselves. Doctrine and discipline were maintained for eight centuries without any aid from Isidore; and for the last two centuries his assistance has been dispensed with, and no change has ensued. Mr. Ffoulkes then has no reason to be anxious about the effect produced by quotations from the False Decretals found in the Oration of the Provincial of the Dominicans in the Council of Florence; in the Letter of Leo IX. to Michael Cerularius; or in the Roman Catechism, which takes its usual name from the Council of Trent. That Catechism was drawn up by theologians who, like all others in that age, were firmly persuaded that the Decretals of the Pontiffs, both before and after Pope Damasus, were authentic; it is not wonderful then if they freely quoted these Decretals along with passages taken from Fathers and Councils. Mr. Ffoulkes frequently manifests surprise at circumstances which have really little in them to account for the impression they produce. Thus, he goes on, as he says, to "call our attention to a more flagrant case." He quotes from the Roman Catechism, q. 6 (not 5, as is printed in the pamphlet), "Pastors are enjoined to teach the Faithful that Christ our Lord instituted the Sacrament of Confirmation, and that He (*teste S. Fabiano Pontifice Romano*) ordered the rite of the chrism and the words which the

Catholic Church uses in its administration." Mr. Ffoulkes is indignant that "the asseverations of such authorities should be taught as Gospel from our pulpits in these days."[1] But what are these asseverations to which allusion is made in the passage quoted from the Roman Catechism? The title of the question is, "Quis Sacramenti Confirmationis sit auctor?" The answer is, that Christ our Lord is the Author of it. But to be author of the Sacrament certainly implies the institution of what is essential to it; that is to say, of the outward symbolical element, and of the words which by divine virtue render it effectual to infuse grace into the soul. Had not Christ instituted the words and the external symbol, He would not be the author of the Sacrament; because it consists of the symbol and the words alone. But this must not be understood as if Christ had in the case of every Sacrament fixed the exact grammatical form of the words, and the precise shape which the symbol was to take; or as the theologians speak, *in specie infima*. But it was necessary that He should have at least established the kind of the symbol to be employed for each individual Sacrament, and, moreover, the chief characteristic idea which the consecratory words were to express. Now the extract given by Mr. Ffoulkes from the Catechism does not say more than this. In fact, immediately after those words it continues: "Quod quidem iis facile probare poterit qui Confirmationem sacramentum esse confitentur, quum sacra omnia mysteria humanæ naturæ vives superent, nec ab alio quam a Deo possint institui." The argument in the Catechism is then as follows: "Confirmation

[1] *The Church's Creed*, p. 33.

being a Sacrament, could not be instituted by any one save by God alone ; but Confirmation consists of a material symbol and of certain words having reference to the effect of the Sacrament ; therefore Christ could not institute it without determining the outward sign, and the words necessary to effect the consecration." Mr. Ffoulkes cannot raise any objection to this. Since the time of the Council of Trent, it has rightly been regarded as heresy to assert that Confirmation, or any other of the seven Sacraments, was instituted in the Church through the Apostles, or *a fortiori* after their age. But it would come to the same thing to assert that the kind of sensible symbol, and the form of words in their general meaning, were not instituted by Christ, but by the Apostles, or in a later age. This is the error which the Catechism directly contradicts by referring to divine institution both the Sacrament of Confirmation and all that goes to make up this Sacrament. In the next question the Catechism speaks of the *materia*, or of the symbolical part of this Sacrament. And then it states that the chrism is the matter of this Sacrament, and alleges for it the authority of several ancient Fathers and Councils. Finally it adds, among other witnesses, Pope Fabian, of whom it says that he has given evidence to the fact that the Apostles were taught the matter of this Sacrament by Christ Himself.

But Mr. Ffoulkes has another charge to make. He goes on to quote some words of Estius: "Plerique opinantur Apostolos in conferendo Confirmationis sacramento chrismate nunquam usos fuisse ;" and hence he declares himself unable to resist the inference that truthfulness is not one of the strongest characteristics of the Church of

Rome.[1] Want of proper theological training may in some manner excuse the blunder here committed. We remark, first, that we are not disposed to admit the assertion of Estius in its full extent; but even admitting it, nothing follows in opposition to the teaching of the Catechism. The Catechism does not say that the Apostles conferred the Sacrament of Confirmation by the sacred chrism; but that they learnt from Christ that chrism was the *materia* of confirmation. These two assertions are far from being contradictory; and they are both held together by many theologians, including St. Thomas and the Synod of Mayence. The controversy will be found treated at length by Witasse.[2]

IX.

But Mr. Ffoulkes is not satisfied with finding the origin of the prerogatives of the Pope in the forgery of the Decretals; he has also made the great discovery that "the Crusades completed the ecclesiastical aggrandisement of the Papacy by force." These are his own words, the words in which he proposes his *thesis*.[3] But what are his proofs? I must confess that I am unable to find any in the two or three declamatory pages of his pamphlet on this subject, nor is more said in the second volume of *Christendom's Divisions*. He tells us that the

---

[1] *The Church's Creed*, p. 33.
[2] Witasse, *Tract. de Confirmatione*, pt. i., quæst. ii., art. iii., sec. 3.
[3] *The Church's Creed*, p. 34.

Crusades "could never have taken place without the Pope." Well? "Therefore," he concludes, "for good and for evil, he (the Pope), stands committed to them in every sense." A very strange inference! And what has this to do with the thesis? He then goes on, that the Crusades, socially considered, carried but little religion or virtue with them into Europe; that politically they proved a fatal mistake for humanity, and opened the door by which the Turks came in. Be it so; but what proof of the thesis have we here? Next the Crusades are looked at ecclesiastically, and our author "can discover no redeeming feature whatever in them from the first to the last." He therefore declaims against the "combination of the Cross with the sword," and the "Bishops who became generals of armies." This is very good, no doubt, but all this, true or false as it may be, does not prove the thesis. Then, after this declamation has been continued for two whole pages, we come, at last, to the great proof of his thesis. "What was attempted by all," he says, "after their first burst of enthusiasm was over, was to subjugate the Churches of the East to that of Rome in the way opposed to the Canons." And he adds that "the researches of Sir Francis Palgrave go far to prove that the Crusades set out with this object." But "at all events," he remarks, "the idea dawned upon them with their first success." "And this was exactly," he concludes, "what Innocent III. completed on the capture of Constantinople." He goes on to assert that Innocent III. committed the most flagrant breach of the Canons by the act of consecrating Thomas Morosini Patriarch of Constantinople, "John Camater, the lawful Patriarch, being alive, and expelled by force, without any previous trial or inquiry;" and the only excuse he can find for Innocent is that he believed in the genuineness of the Decretals. Mr. Ffoulkes, in this part of his pamphlet, has done no more than sum up what the enemies of the Church had said in old times against Pope Innocent, and what he himself had written a year ago in the second part of his *Christendom's Divisions*.[1] But granting all that he has written, would it involve the truth of the thesis, which the author so boldly undertakes to prove in these pages, that the Crusades completed the aggrandisement of the Papacy by force? Mr. Ffoulkes cannot but know that for ten centuries the East and the West had been united in faith and discipline, without any kind of force being necessary to maintain this union under the divinely-conferred jurisdiction of the Pope; and in another place[2] we have given some illustrations of the way in which this jurisdiction was exercised, and we have shown that it was never disputed by any Bishop, Patriarch, or Council. Mr. Ffoulkes says that Innocent III. completed, by the capture of Constantinople, the ecclesiastical aggrandisement of the Papacy. But did he forget that eight centuries before Innocent III., Pope Siricius (with whom the regular series of the Pontifical Letters begins) had solemnly declared that "he was entrusted *with the care of all the Churches*, and that the Roman Church was the head of all."[3] Did he forget that from this Pope down to Innocent III. all the

---

[1] See chs. ii.—iv., pp. 78—227.
[2] *Supreme Authority of the Pope*, secs. iv., v., pp. 81—137.
[3] *Epist.* vi., n. 1 (Coustant, p. 659).

successors of St. Peter had constantly expressed the same conviction, whilst all the Church concurred in the same view, Photius himself not excluded.[1] The power of the Pope was complete from the time when Christ said to Peter: "Thou art Peter, and upon this rock I will build My Church;" and again: "Feed My sheep, feed My lambs." The exercise of Peter's power was to have no other limits than those which are placed to the power of the Church itself. But it is absurd to say that the Papal power was aggrandised or completed because some schismatic or heretical provinces, which had once been in union with the Church, returned again to the centre of Catholic unity and charity. Papal authority is essential to the Church; it is that vital principle by which all the parts of the Church are kept together in one compact body, although, without the spirit of Christ giving life and increase to the whole, this vital principle would be unable to perform its divinely-appointed functions. It is absurd in physiology to say that the vital principle of man receives increase or completeness through the growth and development of the members; and it is no less absurd in theology to speak of the Papal authority as aggrandised because some provinces of the East made their submission to the Chair of St. Peter. A true understanding of this cardinal idea of Catholic unity might have been expected from one who has passed many years in Catholic communion.

We have spoken thus far, assuming the truth of the view put forward by Mr. Ffoulkes of the Crusades. But this view is not a true one; it is a tissue of calumnies, a hundred times brought forward by the enemies of the

[1] See what we have said above upon this subject.

Church, and as often refuted by her apologists. The main charge is that the Popes, and in particular Innocent III., sanctioned the use of force for the purpose of subduing the schismatic Churches of the East to their obedience. We will show that this charge is unfounded. Twelve months before the publication of his pamphlet, Mr. Ffoulkes addressed the world with more reserve than he has now shown. In the pamphlet he exaggerates the evils brought upon the Greeks by the Crusades, intending to heap more odium upon the Popes, without whom, he says, these expeditions could never have taken place. In the second part of his *Christendom's Divisions*, he speaks with approval of the leading Christian idea which inspired the Crusades, and he declares that "this was certainly the idea put forward at the time by those who advocated them—the way in which it was carried out is another question altogether;" and he adds that "it would be most unreasonable to suppose that their early professions were not sincere."[1] He acknowledges that "for two hundred years the East had been calling upon the West for assistance,"[2] and in accordance with this view he does not abstain from praising the idea of the Crusades, and he asserts that "their principal actors advocated a great cause, and one of the holiest wars ever undertaken in self-defence."[3] "There would be no grander page in history had the Crusaders contented themselves with expelling the Turks from Christian soil."[4] The Popes are fully justified if it be admitted that they brought about a series of expeditions for which the Patriarchs and

[1] *Christendom's Divisions*, pt. ii., ch. ii., p. 99.
[2] *Ibid.*, p. 101. [3] *Ibid.*, p. 99. [4] *Ibid.*, p. 100.

people of the East had been begging throughout two hundred years, which would have had the effect of renewing the ties which bound together the great Christian family, of bursting the chains with which the Faithful in the East were held in slavery, of driving back their oppressors, and of once more leaving the way open for the spread of true civilisation. These are the intentions described in *Christendom's Divisions* as held " in perfect sincerity " by the Popes. How, then, has it come to pass that after the lapse of twelve months Mr. Ffoulkes can write as follows in his pamphlet? "What was attempted by all after their first burst of enthusiasm was over, was to subjugate the Churches of the East to that of Rome in a way opposed to the Canons." He refers to "the researches of Sir F. Palgrave, which," as he says, "go far to prove that the Crusaders actually set out with this object."[1] But he was aware that the researches of Sir F. Palgrave, which tend to this conclusion, involve an element of " pure romance."[2] " At all events," he says, " some of the first letters written home by the Crusaders to the Pope who organised them, show that the idea dawned upon them with their first success;"[3] and in proof of this he gives an extract from a letter, the genuineness of which seemed doubtful to him when engaged in his *Christendom's Divisions*,[4] and he omits to tell us that, even admitting the letter to be genuine, it is of little autho-

---

[1] *The Church's Creed*, p. 35.
[2] *Christendom's Divisions*, pt. ii., ch. ii., p. 103.
[3] *Ibid.*, p. 107. "Well he might, if the letter dispatched by Bohemond, Prince of Antioch, and his companions in arms to Urban *is genuine.*"
[4] *Ibid.*

rity, for it was written by Prince Bohemond in a moment of great anger, occasioned by a rumour that the Patriarch of Antioch was preparing to betray the city into the hands of the Greek Emperor.[1] Besides all this, the language of the letter is far from proving the desired point. The writer says that the Crusaders had overcome the Turks, but that they were unable to overcome the heretical Greeks and Armenians, and he goes on: "Only come over to us, and complete that which you have commenced with us, and the whole world will obey you." These words, it is clear, are prompted by anger in the rough heart of a soldier, who was indignant at being deprived of his principality by the treason of the Greek Patriarch. Moreover, it is well known that the fourth Crusade was turned away from its original purpose by accidents which took the leaders by surprise. The need of shipping and want of money first led the Crusaders to assist the Venetians in the reduction of Zara. After the fall of that town they would have started immediately for Palestine, had not the young Alexis IV., son of the Emperor Isaac the Angel, made an appeal to their generous feelings by setting before their eyes the usurpation of Alexis III., and the ignominious and cruel imprisonment of his father, entreating them to take revenge. Constantinople fell indeed into their hands, but they delivered it up to Alexis IV., and proclaimed him Emperor. Had he fulfilled his engagements, and paid the money which he had promised, they would have left Galata and proceeded against the Turks in Palestine. But the most lively indignation was aroused in the breasts of

[1] *Christendom's Divisions*, p. 160.

the Crusaders, first by the breach of faith on the part of the young Emperor, and then by his cruel death, when he was strangled by a new usurper, and they resolved to take revenge, and to turn their arms against the capital of the Byzantine Empire. It is true that, independently of these circumstances, "there was a growing feeling in Europe that the Greeks were at the bottom of all the fortunes of the Latins in the East."[1] Mr. Ffoulkes confesses it, and adds that "the failure of the second Crusade was remembered against the Greeks by the French and Germans." But he does not tell with what insolence the Greek Emperor Emmanuel Comnenus treated the German Conrad, nor how, out of the 70,000 men of the Christian army, 60,000 fell beneath the swords of the Mussulmen through the treachery of the Greek guides. He does not say how with what treacherous arts the Byzantine Emperor tried to ensnare the formidable army of Louis VII., and what subtle efforts he made that it might fall into the ambush laid by the Sultan of Iconium. The third Crusade felt that it had been driven by the Greeks to get to the Holy Land by sea. Barbarossa was obliged to have recourse to open threats in order to save his army from the insidious artifices of the Greek people and Emperor, who would willingly have proclaimed a crusade against the Latins, but were deterred by the strength of the enemy. In fact, under Andronicus, when the Greeks felt superior in force, they slaughtered without distinction all the Latins in Constantinople, reduced their quarter to ashes, and sold above 4,000 of them into perpetual slavery among the

[1] *Christendom's Divisions*, l. c.

Turks. These occurrences happened between the third and fourth Crusades. It is impossible, therefore, to feel surprise at the conduct of the French and Venetians on the capture of Constantinople; the only surprise is that all Christendom did not join in extirpating that den of traitors. The Crusaders deserve rather the praise of Christian forbearance than the blame of a settled design for the conquest of the Greek capital, of which they did not attempt to possess themselves until after the lapse of more than a hundred years, and repeated provocations which would have justified such an enterprise. On this subject the judgment of Gibbon is fairer than that of the writer on whom we are commenting. "It was secretly and perhaps tacitly resolved," he says, "by the Prince and people (Greek) to destroy or at least to discourage the pilgrims by every species of injury and oppression, and their want of prudence and discipline continually afforded the pretence or the opportunity. The Western monarchs had stipulated a safe passage and fair market in the country of their Christian brethren, the treaty had been ratified by oaths and hostages, and the poorest soldier of Frederic's army was furnished with three marks of silver to defray his expenses on the road. But every engagement was violated by treachery and injustice, and the complaints of the Latins are attested by the honest confession of a Greek historian, who has dared to prefer truth to his country. Instead of an hospitable reception, the gates of the cities, both in Europe and Asia, were closely barred against the Crusaders, and the scanty pittance of food was let down in baskets from the walls. Experience or foresight might excuse their jealousy, but the common duties of humanity prohibited the mixture of chalk or other poisonous ingredients in the bread. . . . In every step of their march they were stopped or misled; the governors had private orders to fortify the passes and break down the bridges against them; the stragglers were pillaged and murdered; the soldiers and horses were pierced in the woods by arrows from an invisible hand; the sick were burnt in their beds; and the dead bodies were hung on gibbets along the highways. These injuries exasperated the champions of the Cross, who were not endowed with evangelical patience, and the Byzantine Princes, who had provoked the unequal conflict, promoted the embarcation and march of these formidable guests."[1]

The facts to which Gibbon alludes afford clear proof, that long before the time of the fourth Crusade the arms of the Latins would have been directed against Constantinople, had these not been actuated by a simple desire to expel the Turks from Palestine without staining their hands with Christian blood. Still more clear is it, that from the very beginning of the Crusades the Popes kept this noble purpose alone before their minds, and directed to it all their endeavours; they sought nothing but the emancipation of the holy places, and the liberation of the Christians of Palestine from the sway of the Turks. Mr. Ffoulkes must feel that to support the view which he has put forward, he ought to be prepared with evidence that the Popes proclaimed some Crusade for the purpose of overthrowing the Greek Empire, and reducing the East by force to

[1] *History of the Decline and Fall of the Roman Empire*, ch. lix., n. 2, vol. vii., p. 297, seq. London, 1825.

acknowledge the Papal authority. But no proofs to
this purpose are forthcoming, and particularly in the
case of Innocent III., it is notorious that he was wholly
averse to the capture of Constantinople, which took
place during his reign. What we say is clearly evinced
by the Letters of that great Pope, which, as Mr.
Ffoulkes himself tells us, are still a witness to his inmost
thoughts.[1] As soon as the news arrived that the
Crusaders had undertaken the task of restoring Alexis
to the throne, Innocent wrote to them in great indignation ; he told them that they had not assumed the
Cross for any such purpose, but to do battle with the
Turks ; and he goes on in the same Letter : " Let none
of you be so rash as to presume to spoil or occupy
Greek territory on the pretence that it is not subject
to the Apostolic See." Mr. Ffoulkes quotes this very
Letter, and these very words, in his *Christendom's
Divisions ;*[2] and asserts that " Innocent never once
swerved from the objects expressed in his Encyclic."[3]
He acknowledges the great perplexity of the Pope on
receiving the news of the capture of Constantinople ;
states from his Letters the grounds on which he
accepted the establishment of the new empire, which
he regarded as a work disposed by Divine Providence
in order to obtain and secure the possession of that
country where Christ had worked out our salvation.
The language used by Mr. Ffoulkes in this work is
very different from that found in the pamphlet, where
he speaks of Innocent's conduct as unworthy of the
Head of the Church ; where he denounces the Pope's

[1] *Christendom's Divisions,* pt. ii., ch. iii., p. 168.
[2] *Ibid.,* p. 177. [3] *Ibid.,* p. 176.

violence, hypocrisy, downright profanity, participation in usurped spoils, identification of the Holy See with the outrageousness of the whole proceeding, and closes his invective with the following words: "Who can possibly believe in a God of Justice, and doubt His holding the Papacy heavily responsible for all this?"[1] All this is exactly in the tone of the older Protestant and schismatic writers against Pope Innocent III.; it is merely a repetition of the calumnies which Hurter and many other apologists of that great Pope have successfully refuted.

X.

A few remarks must be added on the charge brought against Innocent in connection with the election of Thomas Morosini to the Patriarchal Chair of Constantinople. It may be stated in the words of Mr. Ffoulkes: "Of all the breaches of the Canons in ecclesiastical history, it would be difficult to find one more flagrant than the act of Innocent in consecrating Morosini Patriarch of Constantinople—John Camater, the rightful Patriarch, being alive, and expelled by force, without any previous trial or inquiry."[2] The same topic is also treated in *Christendom's Divisions*, and the writer twice attributes Innocent's conduct to his belief in the False Decretals.[3] Now we have an unexceptionable witness to the circumstances under which

[1] *The Church's Creed*, p. 36.
[2] *Ibid.*, p. 35, seq.
[3] *Christendom's Divisions*, pt. ii., ch. iv., p. 192, seq.

John Camater left the city in the person of the historian Nicetas, who himself accompanied the Patriarch on the occasion, and yet he tells us nothing of any force being employed. Nicetas tells us that John left the city with a number of families which retired, in order to avoid any risk of insult at the hands of the victorious invaders.[1] But Mr. Ffoulkes tells us that "John Camater was driven out of Constantinople with marked ignominy by the soldiers of the Cross themselves."[2] He took this from Ephraemius, a poet of the fourteenth century, who alone mentions the incident, on which both Nicetas and George Acropolite are silent,[3] and yet the pamphlet quotes no name but that of Nicetas. Further it is to be remarked that after the spontaneous departure of John from Constantinople, he fixed his residence at Didymoticum, leaving the Byzantine see vacant; and being requested by Lascaris to transfer his see to Nicæa, where the Greek imperial court was established, he refused to do so, and resigned his Patriarchate in writing; whereupon one Michael Auctorianus was appointed his successor.[4] We do not allege this by way of justification of the appointment of a Latin Patriarch; it will be sufficient justification to quote the words of Mr. Ffoulkes himself in his *Christendom's Divisions*: "Innocent was no lawless invader of the rights of others, but rather he was one of the most

---

[1] See Nicetas Chron., *Hist. Urbs capta*, n. 5, p. 784 (Edit. Bonn); and Le Quien, *Oriens Christianus*, Appendix; *Patriarchæ Constantinopolitani ritûs Latini*, i. (In t. iii., p. 796); *Acta SS.*, t. i.; Mensis Augusti, *Patriarchæ Constantinop.*, Parergon viii., p. 146.

[2] *Christendom's Divisions*, l. c.

[3] Ephraemius, *De Patriarchis Constant.*, p. 410. Edit. Bonn.

[4] Georgius Acropolita, *Annales*, n. 6, p. 13. Edit. Bonn.

eminent and exact Canonists that ever adorned the Chair of St. Peter; and if he took the loftiest views of the prerogatives of his See, it was because he believed them to be thoroughly consonant with law and equity."[1] The only mistake of Mr. Ffoulkes in this place is his belief that the part taken by Innocent in the election of Morosini was not "consonant with law and equity." Mr. Ffoulkes should place himself in the position of a true Catholic in order to understand this question. True Catholics are fully convinced that the Greek Church is a schismatic body walking in the path of heresy; therefore, now as ever, they regard John Camater as a schismatic Patriarch on the verge of heresy. They open the *Corpus Juris Canonici*, in order to see what kind of punishment is decreed by the Canons against a schismatic Prelate, and they find that he is anathematised *ipso jure*, and deprived of every kind of ecclesiastical power and jurisdiction.[2] These Canons do not derive their origin from the False Decretals, but they belong altogether to authentic sources, and are far anterior to the forgery of the Decretals. They are drawn out of the writings of St. Cyprian, St. Ambrose, St. Jerome, and Pope Pelagius II. It is St. Cyprian who asserts that he who does not keep the unity of the Church has not the ordination of the Church;[3] that he is to be regarded

[1] *Christendom's Divisions*, pt. ii., ch. iv., p. 200.
[2] *Decretum*, pt. ii., caus. vii., q. i., cann. 5, 6, 9, p. 196; caus. xvi., q. vii., can. 19, p. 277; caus. xxiii., q. v., cann. 42, 43, p. 323; caus. xxiv., q. i., cann. 19, 23, 31, 34, pp. 333, 335, seq. (In *Corpore Juris Canonici*, t. i. Edit. a Pithæo. Lipsiæ, 1695).
[3] "Non habet ecclesiasticam ordinationem qui Ecclesiæ non tenet unitatem" (*Epist.* lii. *ad Antonianum*, p. 68. Edit. Balutii).

as an alien, a profane person, and an enemy;[1] that he who refuses the unity and the peace of the Episcopate cannot have the power and the honour of a Bishop;[2] that all heretics and schismatics are deprived of all their power and jurisdiction.[3] The other writers mentioned above, and especially St. Jerome and Pelagius II., express the same principles of ecclesiastical legislation. Hence, according to the ancient laws of the Catholic Church, a Bishop who separated himself from the centre of unity was *ipso jure* excommunicated and deprived of power and jurisdiction. But John Camater was regarded by the Catholic Church as a schismatic Bishop; therefore he was looked upon as being under anathema, and devoid of all episcopal jurisdiction, notwithstanding his Canonical election; and this too according to the ancient laws of the Byzantine Patriarchate.

It must be further added, that John Camater proved obstinate in his schism, and favourable to heresies spread in the Eastern Church about that time by a Monk named Sicidites against the incorruptibility of the Body of Christ in the Sacrament of the Eucharist. Nicetas himself bears witness to the truth of this latter charge.[4] Innocent III., from the very beginning of his

---

[1] "Alienus est, profanus est, hostis est," &c. (*De Unitate Ecclesiæ*, p. 195).

[2] "Episcopi nec potestatem habere potest neque honorem qui Episcopatûs nec unitatem voluit tenere nec pacem" (*Epist.* lii., cit., p. 74).

[3] "Dicimus omnes omnino hæreticos et schismaticos nihil habere potestatis et juris" (*Epist.* lxxvi. *ad Magnum*, p. 151).

[4] Nicetas, Op. cit., *De Alexio Isaaci Angeli fratre*, l. iii., p. 681, seq. Edit. Bonn.

Pontificate, had used every exertion to induce John Camater to return to the bond of unity, but his efforts were unavailing against the hypocritical duplicity of the Greek.[1] Afterwards, when the capital fell into the hands of the Latins, the Patriarch withdrew from his see, evidently in order not to be forced to submit to the supreme authority of the Pope, to whom John seems to have promised submission even by an oath[2] when the Crusaders restored Alexis IV. to the throne of Constantinople. He survived the fall of the Byzantine capital for two years, but he did not make any overtures for a reconciliation with Rome, and he died in his schism. In the meanwhile, the Church of Constantinople returned to the centre of ecclesiastical unity, and with it several of the dependent Churches. It was then necessary to appoint a new Catholic Patriarch, who should restore the independence of the Greek Church (then lying ignominiously prostrate under the power of the Emperor) and strengthen its ties with Rome. And the need of this is the more evident when we remember the Divine and Apostolic institution in the Church that the people who are separate from their Bishop are separate from the Body of Christ, and have no share in His Sacrifice. This is the teaching of St. Cyprian.[3] Now John Camater was not only himself in obstinate

[1] See *Innocentii Papæ Gesta*, n. lxii., seq. (*PP. LL.*, t. cxiv., p. cxxiii. Edit. Migne).

[2] See *Acta SS.*, t. i., Aug.; *Hist. Chron. Patriarch. Constant.*, n. 875, p. 146.

[3] "Plebs obsequens Prælatis Dominicis et Deum metuens, a peccatore præposito separare se debet, nec se ad sacrilegi sacerdotis sacrificia miscere" (S. Cyprianus, *Epist.* lxviii., p. 118. Edit. Balutii).

schism, but in order to persevere in it, he had not scrupled to desert his see, and give up the care of his people; and this conduct alone deprived him of any claim to his Patriarchal dignity. Mr. Ffoulkes confesses that Innocent III. was an "exact Canonist," and no "lawless invader of the rights of others;" and when the Pope heard of the election of Thomas Morosini, he annulled the election on the ground of its not having been made according to the prescription of the Canons. Afterwards, in virtue of his supreme power, he chose the same Morosini to be Patriarch of Constantinople. But neither when he declared the first appointment null, nor when he subsequently confirmed it, did he make any mention of John Camater. Nor is any remark upon the case made by writers of the time, although all notice that the Greek Patriarch was still living when Thomas Morosini was placed in his chair. This proves first, that the election of the new Patriarch was not considered an infraction of any Canon; secondly, that it is a mere dream to say that Innocent III. acted in that manner because "he believed in the genuineness of the Pseudo-Decretals," "which extended the Patriarchate of Rome over the whole East."[1] There is absolutely no foundation for this idea. Nowhere in the False Decretals is authority given to the Pope to depose a Patriarch without trial or formal sentence: yet this was done in the case of John Camater. We must therefore conclude that Innocent III., after the capture of Constantinople, and the known conduct of the Greek Patriarch, manifestly ignored him altogether, and

[1] *The Church's Creed*, p. 36; *Christendom's Divisions*, pt. ii., ch. iv., p. 200.

considered the Byzantine see as vacant, and as standing in need of a Catholic Pastor, on account of the submission of the new empire to the Apostolic See. But when he acted thus his conduct was "thoroughly consonant with law and equity."

XI.

WE trust that we have said enough to cut away the root of the argument by which Mr. Ffoulkes, in his recent pamphlet, endeavours to construct some apology for the Oriental and Anglican schisms. The very purpose for which the pamphlet was written appears to have been the justification of the latter schism, and the support of that system of "branch churches" which is advocated by the party which recognises Dr. Pusey as its head. The author says that some years ago he looked upon the argument of the late Archdeacon Wilberforce against the Church of England as unanswerable—that the West had no right at all in legislating for itself, to innovate upon the existing and unrepealed ordinances of the whole Church.[1] Again, he confesses that he once regarded the position of the Church of England as the effect of schism—wilful and deliberate schism, and he expressed this view unhesitatingly in the first part of his *Christendom's Divisions*.[2] But, he continues, having since discovered the general system of Church government in which England, in common with all other Western nations, had up to that time

[1] *The Church's Creed*, p. 26.　　[2] *Ibid.*, p. 59.

acquiesced, to have been based upon forgeries and opposed to the genuine Code of the Church, he as unhesitatingly recognises the right, nay, the paramount duty of every local Church to revolt against such a concatenation of spurious legislation as this, and scattering to the winds every link of the deceptive chain by which it has been so long enthralled, to return to the letter and spirit of those genuine Canons, stamped with the assent of the whole Church, and never repealed.[1] In a word, Mr. Ffoulkes thinks that the Church of England was right in separating itself from Rome, because it discovered that the authority of the Pope was the result of spurious Decretals, and consequently was not binding on it. This line of reasoning admits of several answers. First, the statement of Mr. Ffoulkes is wholly groundless. The beginning of the Anglican schism dates from 1531, when Henry VIII. set up an ecclesiastical supremacy in his own person, as a step to that discarding of the Papal supremacy, which took place as early as 1534, by the King's proclamation.[2] Now, although in the fifteenth century Nicholas Cusanus and John Turrecremata had believed the Decretals ascribed to the early Popes to be false, nevertheless their opinion did not find followers, nor did it spread. The complete edition of the False Decretals published by Merlin in 1524, and 1530, in Paris and Cologne, was everywhere received with the greatest satisfaction and praise. It was in the course of the fifteenth century that a suspicion of their spuriousness began to gain ground, by the works published in Germany by George Cassandre in 1564,

[1] L. c.   [2] See it in Wilkins, *Conc. Brit.*, vol. iii., p. 772.

and in France by Dumoulin in 1570, in which it was critically proved that the Isidorian Decretals were a forgery. But their spuriousness was not universally admitted until the time of Blondel, and especially of the two Ballerinis. Now Blondel published his book in the seventeenth century, and the Ballerinis not till the middle of the eighteenth. How is it, then, that Henry VIII., in 1531, was convinced of the spuriousness of Papal legislation, and discarded the Papal supremacy as grounded on forgery? Mr. Ffoulkes agrees with the Anglicans of the old school, and attributes the act of separation from the centre of Catholic unity to the Church of England, whilst the Anglican Church was nothing but a puppet in the hands of an ambitious King and of a more ambitious Queen. The fault of the Church of England was having made itself the slave of Henry and Elizabeth. And it was for this that it cast off the ties of union and submission to the Apostolic See. Where did Mr. Ffoulkes find that the Clergy of England, either when being entangled in a *præmunire* by Henry VIII., they recognised the King's headship in the Church of England, or when as *mutum armentum* they signed the King's proclamation against the Papal supremacy, were persuaded to adopt this course by the great discovery of the forgery of the Decretals? It is amusing to contrast the mean spirit really exhibited during the progress of the Anglican schism with the high-minded views attributed to the Clergy by our pamphleteer.[1] But, moreover, we have proved at length that the

[1] See on this subject the *Supreme Authority of the Pope*, Concl., p. 210, seq.

supremacy of the Popes all over the Church, with all prerogatives belonging to it, were claimed, exercised, and acknowledged long before the time when the False Decretals appeared; and we have shown that this supremacy no way depends upon that forgery, but is derived from the institution of our Divine Saviour Himself. It follows that all the reasoning of Mr. Ffoulkes in defence of the Anglican schism is baseless, and topples to the ground. The Anglican Church for many centuries had joined with the rest of the Catholic world in recognising the supreme authority of the Pope, as was done in the two Synods of Arles and Sardica, but the Prelates of that Church submitted, like foolish sheep, to be enslaved under the tyrannical power of Henry VIII. and Elizabeth, rejecting and condemning this divine authority, and they acted thus in order to please their Prince, who had received from God no authority whatever to lead and govern the Church. This is the plain historical fact, and it constitutes an evident case of schism.

But Mr. Ffoulkes, not content with attacking in this manner the supremacy of the Popes over the Church of England, makes an assault even on their Patriarchal rights over it. "Even the act," he says, "of St. Augustine and his companions, in establishing the jurisdiction of the Patriarch of the West over this island is found illegal, having been declared null and void by anticipation in the Eighth Canon of the Council of Ephesus."[1] Now what is the force of this Canon of Ephesus, to which Mr. Ffoulkes, following in the wake of many Anglican writers, makes so

---

[1] *The Church's Creed*, p. 59, seq.

confident an appeal? The Bishops of Cyprus, availing themselves of the Eustathian schism, had emancipated themselves from the Patriarchal jurisdiction of Antioch, and constituted the *autocephalia* of their Metropolitan. When the schism was healed they refused to return to their ancient Patriarchal submission, and they paid no attention to the complaints of the Patriarch of Antioch, nor even to the exhortations of Pope Innocent I.[1] The Patriarch laid claim at Ephesus to the ordination of the Bishops of Cyprus. But Reginus, Metropolitan of that island, persuaded the assembled Fathers that his Church had since the beginning enjoyed the privilege of Patriarchal independence, and obtained from the Synod a favourable Decree. Thereupon the Council enacted that no Bishop should assume any other province that is not, or was not formerly and from the beginning, subject to him or to those who were his predecessors, and it declared null and of no force any contrary regulation. Now, what has that Canon to do with the Canonical independence of England, and its freedom from subjection to the Roman Patriarch? Mr. Ffoulkes seems much embarrassed in treating this matter. He says:[2] "It is idle or worse than idle to assert that St. Augustine found England subject to Rome when he arrived. It is quite true that he accomplished its submission two centuries and a half or more previously to the publication of the Pseudo-Decretals, but it is no less true that its subjection was accomplished in the teeth of this Canon, as well as of the protest of the native Episcopate that he

[1] *Epist.* xxiv., cap. iii. (Coustant, p. 852).
[2] *The Church's Creed*, p. 59, seq.

found in possession." Mr. Ffoulkes seems to admit that at the date of the arrival of St. Augustine in England the British Church was already subject to the Patriarchal jurisdiction of the Roman See ; but if this be so, it must be admitted that this subjection could be brought about without any breach of the Canon of Ephesus. No other Church can be meant than that of the Britons, confined to Cornwall, Wales, and Cumberland, for this was the only Christian community existing in the island at the date of the arrival of St. Augustine in Kent. The Anglo-Saxons, in their various tribes, all followed the worship of Woden, until St. Augustine succeeded in converting the King of Kent, from which district the faith gradually spread into the neighbouring kingdoms. St. Augustine had received episcopal consecration at the hands of some French Bishops in the very first year of his mission, but he received from Pope St. Gregory the see of Canterbury, with metropolitical power over the twelve suffragan sees which embraced the southern portion of the Saxon dominions. The northern districts were placed under the authority of the Archbishop of York, to whom also the same number of twelve suffragans was assigned ; and it was arranged that as long as St. Augustine lived, he should exercise jurisdiction even over the see of York and the northern province. Thus the new Church owed to the Pope the whole of its organisation, the names of the episcopal cities, and their subordination. Nor was force or violence employed in procuring this result, nor was it any way necessary.[1] On the other hand, as we have seen, Mr. Ffoulkes confesses that the British Church was

[1] V. Beda, *Hist. Eccl.*, L i., cap. xxix., p. 76, seq. Londini, 1838.

subject to the Patriarchal jurisdiction of Rome at the time of St. Augustine's arrival, and we shall see directly that this subjection dated back to the very first foundation of that Church. This jurisdiction was therefore perfectly legitimate and in force throughout the whole of what is now called England.

It is true that, owing to the isolated position of the British Church, which after the Saxon invasion was cut off from all free intercourse with the Catholic world, its discipline became much relaxed, and the standard of morals sank very low, through the influence of the example set by the pagan conquerors; but still the Britons held fast to all the articles of the orthodox faith, and amongst the rest to the belief that St. Peter was the only source of all priestly authority in the Church.[1] Nevertheless, it was not a matter of astonishment if the Bishops of the Britons looked with no favourable eye upon the appointment of St. Augustine, with extensive jurisdiction over themselves as well as over the Saxon converts. St. Augustine was reputed severe in his government, and to him was committed the unpopular task of curbing the license which had crept in during times of past disorder. The appointment was regarded as a novelty unknown in the old institutions of the Church, and as a disgraceful badge of subjection to the hated Saxon conqueror; yet all the opposition raised fails to prove that the British Prelates refused to recognise the right of the Pope, or that they withdrew themselves from his obedience. Instances are found, in ancient and modern history alike, in which Catholic Bishops have offered

[1] Gildas, *Epistola*, p. 116. Edit. of Stevenson.

strenuous opposition to particular measures adopted by the Pope in reference to local discipline. The conduct of the African Bishops in the affair of Apiarius furnishes one illustration; another is found in the case of the French Prelates who disapproved of the course adopted by Pius VII. in his negotiations with Napoleon. The British Bishops felt great dislike to the subjection of their own Metropolitan to the authority of a foreigner who occupied the see of Canterbury; moreover, partly out of ignorance and partly through selfish stubbornness in refusing to give up any part of their old customs, they made great difficulty in abandoning their mode of computing Easter, and also in adopting the Roman rite in the administration of Baptism. Enmity to their Saxon oppressors was the motive which determined them not to accept the offer made them by St. Augustine to join with him in preaching the Gospel to the German pagans. The resistance offered to St. Augustine proceeded, then, from particular causes, and is no proof of independence of the Roman Patriarch. In fact, the jurisdiction of the See of Rome is proved by the mere fact of the appointment of St. Augustine with so extensive authority by Pope Gregory. What this great Pope did was not, as Mr. Ffoulkes says, "what St. Leo the Great informed the East the Canons would not allow," &c.,[1] but it was what his predecessor, Celestine I., had done two centuries before in the case of the Scotch Church, when he appointed the Monk Palladius to the government of that community.[2] By

[1] *The Church's Creed*, p. 60.
[2] V. Beda, *Hist. Eccl.*, l. i., cap. xiii., p. 31 (Edit. cit.); S. Prosper, in *Chronico*, an. 431 (In Op., p. 744. Parisiis, 1711).

this act Pope Celestine exercised Patriarchal authority over the Scots, and St. Gregory the Great, treading in his footsteps, showed evidently that his See had always regarded the British Church as comprised within the boundaries of the Western Patriarchate.

But Mr. Ffoulkes is not without some sort of defence for the position which he has taken up; let us examine its strength. He quotes a certain protest of the British Episcopate; and he remarks that "it may well be doubted whether St. Gregory was ever properly made acquainted with their prescriptive claims."[1] Undoubtedly Gregory the Great was never made acquainted with a protest which had no existence whatever in his times. The famous document was first published by Spelman,[2] and honoured by Wilkins with a place in his Collection of the English Councils.[3] Hammond,[4] Bramhall,[5] Collier,[6] and Stillingfleet,[7] grounded upon it their defence of the separation of the English Church from Rome, and their exculpation of their own communion from the crime of schism. The writers whom we have named do not rank high as critics, and we need not wonder that they were deceived; but it is a matter of surprise that the learned Bingham accepted the protest as genuine, and, without making any investi-

---

[1] *The Church's Creed*, p. 60.
[2] *Concilia Orbis Britannici*, p. 108. Londini, 1639.
[3] *Concilia Magnæ Britanniæ*, vol. i., p. 26, seq. Londini, 1737.
[4] *A Defence of the Church of England from Schism*, ch. vi., n. 5, seq. (Op., vol. ii., p. 256, seq. Oxford, 1849).
[5] *A just Vindication of the Church of England*, pt. i., dis. ii., n. 4 (Op., vol. i., p. 162, seq. Oxford, 1842).
[6] *Eccl. Hist. of Great Britain*, bk. ii., vol. i., p. 76.
[7] *Antiquit. Brit.*, p. 360. London, 1685.

gation into its merit, published it as a proof of the independence and metropolitical *autocephalia* of the British Church.[1] At the present day there can be no reasonable doubt that this protest of Abbot Dinorth is a mere forgery, and is rejected not only by Catholic,[2] but by Protestant writers, both in England and elsewhere. Gieseler, without any reserve, terms it a spurious document;[3] and he refers to the authority of Dr. Döllinger and of Mr. Stevenson, the Protestant editor of the historical works of Bede. Although Mr. Stevenson is now a Catholic, he was a Protestant at the time of publishing the work from which we quote; he speaks of the declaration in the following terms: "It is obviously the production of a comparatively recent period, probably not earlier than the reign of Henry VI., and consequently *not entitled to the slightest credit.*"[4] The judgment of Mr. Stevenson carries with it so great a weight of authority, that it dispenses us from quoting

[1] *Christian Antiq.*, bk. ii., ch. xviii., sec. ii., vol. i., p. 248. London.

[2] The first in England to detect the forgery of that document was Turberville, a Catholic, in 1654, and he pointed it out in an article inserted in his *Manual of Controversies*, published in that very year at Douay (See the Appendix, p. 401, seq.). After Turberville, all Catholic writers rejected the spurious Declaration. See for instance Lingard (*The Antiq. of the Anglo-Saxon Church*, ch. ii., n. 9, p. 67. Newcastle, 1806); Dodd (*Church Hist. of England*, art. i., n. 1, p. 26, vol. i. London, 1839); Canon Flanagan (*Hist. of the Church of England*, ch. vi., p. 39, in note. London, 1857). Among foreign writers we can mention two of the most learned—Pagi (*Crit. Bar.*, an. 604, n. viii., t. ii., p. 723. Edit. Antwerpiæ, 1727), and Schelestrate (*Diss. against Ed. Stillingfleet*, ch. vi., p. 92, seq. London, 1688).

[3] *Comp. of Eccl. Hist.*, div. ii., ch. vi., sec. 126, vol. ii., p. 166, seq. Edinburgh, 1848.

[4] V. Beda, *Hist. Eccl.*, sec. 94, n. 6, p. 102. Edit. by Stevenson.

writers upon the point. Nor need we examine all the internal and external marks of forgery found in this Declaration, for they have been fully examined by others,[1] who have pointed out that the original instrument is found without name or date, that its language is quite modern Welsh, and that it calls Caerleon the metropolitan see, although the Archbishopric had been transferred to Menevia, or St. David's, about a century earlier. And even if the protest had been only doubtful, still so doubtful an instrument could not fairly be quoted in controversy, as is done by Mr. Ffoulkes, without a hint of any doubt having been cast upon its authority. Until the doubt is cleared up, the document is of no controversial value whatever. Mr. Ffoulkes is deservedly severe upon Isidore for bringing forward Decretal Letters which he knew to be forgeries. Mr. Ffoulkes can defend himself against the same charge only by avowing great ignorance of the matters on which he has undertaken to write.

Having disposed of this protest, we will resume our main argument regarding the relations between the ancient British Church and Rome. No documents exist which prove the metropolitan independence of the British Bishops; but in the scarcity of direct evidence, many historical facts can be quoted which go to prove their original subjection. The British Church owes its origin to Pope Eleutherius.

[1] See the authors quoted in the last three notes, to whom we may add the late Dr. Ives, formerly Protestant Bishop of South Carolina, who in his *Trials of a Mind* (ch. xix., p. 209, note. London, 1854) has some very good remarks on this subject, taken from an eminent Welsh scholar.

Beda relates that "Lucius, King of the Britons, sent a letter to Pope Eleutherius, that by his orders he might become a Christian. His request was satisfied without delay; and the Britons kept their faith undefiled, in peace and calmness, till the age of Diocletian."[1] The statement of Venerable Beda is fully confirmed by the *Liber Landavensis*, which in two places chronicles the same fact. We there read that "King Lucius sent a letter, and despatched his two ambassadors, Elfan and Medwey, to Pope Eleutherius, imploring that according to his admonition, he might be made a Christian. The Pope acceded to his request, and caused the ambassadors to be baptised; and on their embracing the Catholic faith, Elfan was ordained a Bishop, and Medwey a Doctor. Lucius and the nobles of all Britain received baptism; and according to the command of St. Eleutherius, the Pope, he constituted an ecclesiastical Order, ordained Bishops, and taught the way of leading a good life."[2] Moreover, in the same *Liber Landavensis* we find other important passages which bear on our subject. The writer, in speaking of the privileges of the Church of Llandaff declares that they were "confirmed by Apostolical authority;" and again, "ordained by Apostolical authority;" and finally, in a document whose original text is in Welsh, we read the following words concerning the same Church: "This is the law and privilege of the Church of Teilo of Llandaff, which these Kings and Princes of Wales granted to the

---

[1] *Hist. Eccl.*, l. i., cap. iv., p. 16. Edit. cit.
[2] *Liber Landavensis. Llyfr Teilo*, pp. 26, 65. In the transl., ch. i., p. 306; ch. ii., p. 310. Edit. by W. J. Rees. Llandovery, 1840.

Church of Teilo, and to all its Bishops after him for ever, and was confirmed by the Popes of Rome."[1] We have here clear proof that the foundations of the British Church were laid by the Pope, who from the very beginning exercised over it that Patriarchal authority which was his right. Moreover, when the British Church was threatened with the introduction of heresy by Agricola, the son of Severianus, a Pelagian Bishop, it was Pope Celestine who, at the request of Palladius, dispatched Germanus, Bishop of Auxerre, in order to preserve in its integrity the faith of the people of Britain.[2] Since, then, the whole of England and Wales was subject to the Roman Patriarchate from the very beginning of Christianity among the people, it is impossible to urge the Canon of Ephesus as impeaching the validity of this jurisdiction; and there is no support for the assertion of Mr. Ffoulkes, that the primatial see of England, whether at Caerleon or elsewhere, was originally independent and autocephalous. Let us conclude. The British Church not only recognised the Pope as the Supreme Head of the Universal Church in the two Synods of Arles and Sardica, but also it

---

[1] L. c., cap iii., p. 111, seq., et p. 113.
[2] S. Prosper, in *Chronico*, an. 429 (In Op., p. 744. Edit. Parisiis, 1711); in *Libro Contra Collatorem*, cap. xxi., n. 2, l. c., p. 363. V. Beda (*Hist. Eccl.*, l. i., cap. xvii., p. 38. Edit. cit.) and the *Liber Landavensis* (p. 66. In transl., ch. ii., p. 310) seem to assert that Germanus was sent by the Bishops of France into England. But the authority of St. Prosper is irrefragable, on account of his having been a contemporary writer and secretary of the very Pope who sent Germanus to Britain. As to the manner of reconciling the two apparently contradictory statements, see the work *England and Rome*, by the Rev. W. Waterworth, S.J., ch. v., p. 143, n. 1.

acknowledged him as its own Patriarch, invested with that Canonical jurisdiction which the Roman Patriarch has ever exercised over all the West.

XII.

It now remains to speak as briefly as possible of the Eastern schism. A whole volume might be occupied with the examination of all that Mr. Ffoulkes has advanced on this subject, both in his pamphlet and in the second part of *Christendom's Divisions*, but this would be beyond our present purpose. We will content ourselves with indicating the principal errors put forward so confidently in the Letter to Archbishop Manning. Mr. Ffoulkes begins by remarking "that although Rome may have never erred from the faith in point of dogma, she has trifled with it on one point in practice so often for the last thousand years that her conduct has been a stumbling-block to others, and occasioned a division of the Eastern and Western Churches on doctrinal grounds. Secondly, that by allowing the primitive Code of the Church to be stealthily supplanted by a new Code based upon forgeries, which she accepted without examination, and endeavoured to make binding on others by violence, she has occasioned a division of the Eastern and Western Churches on disciplinary grounds."[1] He declares with great simplicity "that he is not aware that any demur to this conclusion in theory can be raised even by maximisers."

[1] *The Church's Creed*, p. 37.

Now we assert that not only all Catholics, but also every one who is fully acquainted with ecclesiastical history, must condemn these two statements of Mr. Ffoulkes as absolutely false. There is no ground for attributing "to the flagrant unfaithfulness and injustice of the governmental policy of Rome, both as regards doctrine and discipline, the secession of the Eastern Church from her communion."[1] History teaches that it is to be ascribed to the degeneracy, ambition, and pride of the Eastern Church itself, as is done by Dr. Döllinger and many other writers.[2] Mr. Ffoulkes, who has given a long time to the study of Christendom's divisions, especially in relation to the Greek Church, ought to have known better what were the true causes of the Eastern schism, and not to have taken appearances for realities, and his own fancies for actual truths. The reader of the pamphlet might naturally require some proofs to be given that the addition of the word *Filioque* to the Nicene Creed occasioned a division of the Eastern and Western Churches on doctrinal grounds. But none is given, while, in other places, Mr. Ffoulkes has clearly stated his belief that political, and not theological, causes led to the schism. Thus he declares in his *Christendom's Divisions* that "there had been differences in doctrine between the Eastern and Western Churches without producing any schism at all; that other causes were in operation when the schism commenced, and that it was concurrently with the growth of these causes that it advanced to consum-

---

[1] *The Church's Creed*, p. 37.
[2] *History of the Church*, pt. iii., sec. viii., p. 82, seq. London, 1841.

mation, leaving those doctrinal differences, notwithstanding the warmth with which they have been discussed on both sides, exactly where they were when it began."[1] He adds that "there was no fresh theological controversy discussed between Photius and the Pope," and that up to the time when the Encyclic of Photius appeared, not a word had been breathed respecting any charges against the Latins.[2] Further on he remarks that "Photius, in one of his letters, actually dwells on the great diversity of usages in East and West, *with the* purpose of showing that where no doctrine was at stake, nor any Decree of the Catholic world violated, people would do very wrong to condemn others," &c.[3] But Mr. Ffoulkes refers the famous Encyclic of Photius, with its list of charges against the Latins, to the submission of Bulgaria to the Roman Patriarchate, and he qualifies this declaration as "a political manifesto."[4] The Greeks were full of anxiety to make the kingdom of Bulgaria their own, and therefore they esteemed the influence acquired by the Latins as a great misfortune, and as a serious obstacle to their designs. As to the consummation of the Greek schism under Michael Cerularius, Mr. Ffoulkes thinks that this also is to be ascribed to the ambition of Rome, which led to the attempt to substitute Latin influence for Greek in the country now known as Apulia. In a word, he regards the schism as wholly due to the embitterment of feeling produced in the minds of the Greeks on account of the destruction of their influence in Southern Italy by the Norman conquests in Apulia

[1] Pt. ii., ch. i., vol. ii., p. 3.
[2] *Ibid.*, p. 4. [3] *Ibid.*, l. c. [4] *Ibid.*, p. 13.

and Calabria. Many Greeks remained in these districts after the conquest, and they used every effort to preserve their old rites and usages, in order to place greater difficulty in the way of the settled establishment of the Latin invaders; and in this state of popular feeling Mr. Ffoulkes finds an explanation of the letter addressed by Michael Cerularius to the Bishop of Trani, by which the schism was finally completed.[1] Lastly, Mr. Ffoulkes, after having reviewed the facts connected with the Eastern schism, asks: "What do facts show that the whole controversy really turned upon—the primacy, by divine right, of the See of Rome over all Churches in the world ? Nothing of the kind. That primacy was, on the contrary, never once disputed when party spirit was at its highest, and when Rome was, territorially speaking, at its lowest."[2]

Setting together what Mr. Ffoulkes teaches as to the origin of the Eastern schism, we find some inaccuracy in the peculiar views put forward concerning the facts, but it is at least clear that the writer of *Christendom's Divisions* does not trace the cause of the schism to any theological controversies respecting the doctrine of the double procession of the Holy Ghost, or concerning the prerogatives of the Roman Pontiff. And yet an entirely different view is upheld in the pamphlet. There can be little doubt which view is the more correct. From the time when the seat of the imperial power was fixed at Byzantium, the inhabitants of this "New Rome" began to regard the elder city with no little jealousy, and especially the Patriarchs endeavoured to make amends to themselves

[1] *Christendom's Divisions*, p. 23, seq.   [2] *Ibid.*, p. 45.

for their own servile subjection to the tyranny of a godless Court, by reducing under their authority the ancient Patriarchates of Alexandria and Antioch, hoping thus to gain in the East an influence not less than that possessed by Rome in the West. The existence of this spirit explains the Twenty-eighth Canon of Chalcedon, and its rejection by St. Leo the Great;[1] it explains the language in which St. Gregory condemned the title of Ecumenical when assumed by John the Faster and his successors at Constantinople;[2] and the endless series of disputes, discussions, and partial schisms which arose in connection with the doctrine of the Incarnation are explained in the same manner. About the end of the seventh century new causes of discord began to have weight. The Trullan Synod covertly insinuated the entire independence of the East in matters of discipline; this Assembly condemned the practice of ecclesiastical celibacy and of the fast on Saturday, and enacted several other Canons entirely out of harmony with the laws of the Universal Church; and accordingly, the Papal sanction which was asked by Justinian II. was consistently refused to these Canons. The reigns of Leo the Isaurian and of Constantine Copronymus gave rise to new dissensions. These Princes instituted a cruel persecution against the worshippers of sacred images, and their heresy and tyranny alienated the hearts of their subjects in the Italian provinces, who found no resource but to place themselves under the obedience of the Pope and the protection of the

---

[1] See the *Supreme Authority of the Pope*, sec. iv., n. vi., seq., p. 94, seq.
[2] *Ibid.*, sec. iii., n. vii., seq., p. 76, seq.

Frankish Princes. This secession inflicted a great blow upon the already enervated Eastern empire, and in a corresponding measure added to the rising strength of the vigorous nations of the West, and it was not long before the renewal of the Western empire under Charlemagne for the support and protection of the Pope, inflicted a yet severer blow, and for ever destroyed the influence of the Byzantine Court in the Latin provinces.

These political causes of dissension were far from totally destroying the yearning of the people of the East for the Catholic unity of Rome: this is proved by the history of the Second Council of Nicæa. But the seed of evil was sown, and could not fail sooner or later to bring forth its fruit of final separation. Photius sought support in his schemes of ambition from the influence of the Pope; and had Nicholas I. complied with his demands, the open outburst of the schism might have been delayed for a while. But the Pope would not be used as a tool by his aspiring subject, and the schismatical ambition of the Byzantine Patriarch brought on him the sentence of deposition and degradation from his clerical rank; nor were the menaces of the Emperor Michael powerful to set his favourite free from this sentence. In these circumstances it was natural that Photius should look for support to the national jealousies of the Greeks; and he gladly inflamed their prejudices against his enemies by setting before them the submission of Bulgaria to the Pope, as a manifest proof of encroaching ambition on the part of Rome. Here we have the explanation of the origin of the Encyclic of Photius, with its long list of charges against the Western Church;[1] and the publication of this indictment was followed up by a Synod held in Constantinople, in which Photius, like a second Dioscorus, condemned and excommunicated the Pope. It is undoubtedly true that the submission of Bulgaria tended in the highest degree to exasperate Photius and the Greeks in general; but we cannot agree with Mr. Ffoulkes that this submission constituted a starting-point of the schism of the East; it was used by Photius as an instrument for increasing the already existing dislike and jealousy of the authority and usages of Rome. All the charges against the Latins mentioned in the Photian Encyclic were calculated to excite a strong feeling of hostility in the people, and to prepare the way to a complete separation; but it is impossible to consider the calumnies of Photius as the causes of the separation which he determined to bring about in revenge for his own deposition by the Papal authority. He was determined to preserve his Patriarchal dignity at all costs, and his charges against the West afforded him the readiest means of doing so. In fact, as soon as the Emperor Basil, successor to Michael, executed the Papal sentence, and restored Ignatius to the Patriarchal see, the schism was quenched. The supreme and universal authority of the Roman Pontiff was solemnly proclaimed by the Emperor, by the Patriarch, and by all the Episcopate and Clergy of the Eastern Church in the Fourth Synod of Constantinople, which was the Eighth Ecumenical Council, A.D. 869. It is true that jealousy and distrust

[1] *Epist.*, l. i., ep. xiii., *Encyclica Epist.* (Op., t. ii., p. 722, seq. Edit. Migne).

were still shown by the Greeks when treating of the affairs of Bulgaria, for these were mixed up with the political interests of the empire ; but in all the Acts of the Eighth Council there is not a word respecting the charges brought by Photius against the Latins, nor about the introduction of the *Filioque* into the Creed. The proceedings of the Eighth Session,[1] however, do show us something of the iniquitous arts by which Photius had supported his attempt to bring about a formal schism. We read of the five calumnious books forged by Photius against Pope Nicholas; the adherence and subscriptions he had obtained by force and fraud from the Clergy and the laity of every condition ; the falsified signatures to the Acts of the Conciliabulum, in the names of persons who were actually not present. These were the true means which gave rise to the schism ; but nothing is heard of all that to which Mr. Ffoulkes ascribes it, the trifling of the Popes with the dogma of the Procession of the Holy Ghost, and their headlong acceptance of the False Decretals.

From the time of the second deposition of Photius no more was heard of his charges against the Latins, or at least, they were no longer insisted on as an excuse for separation. Luitprand, Bishop of Cremona, in his embassy to Constantinople on behalf of the Emperor Otho, heard nothing of the accusations once raised by Photius. The fact is, that the communion of the Greek with the Roman Church continued to last for nearly two hundred years, dating from the Photian separation. The Greeks it is true, puffed up with pride, jealousy, and corruption, were constantly on the point of a

[1] Conc. Const. iv., Act. viii. (Labbe, t. x., p. 855, seq.).

schism, as had been the case for centuries; but the final schism under Michael Cerularius is to be attributed solely to the insatiable ambition and equal ignorance and pride of that Patriarch, who began by conspiring against his Emperor, and then organised a more formidable conspiracy against the Church. The Encyclic of Photius found its parallel in the letter .of Cerularius to the Bishop of Trani, which was really addressed to the Clergy of France and to the Pope himself, and which gave the signal for revolt and schism. It contains no hint of any of those grievances to which Mr. Ffoulkes would have us ascribe the separation of the East and the West. It deals only with usages more or less important, but none of them essential to the Catholic dogma. Cerularius mentions the unleavened bread in the Eucharist, the fast on Saturdays in Lent, the eating blood and things strangled, and finally, the omission to sing Alleluia on fasting days. No mention of the *Filioque* occurs in the letter; it finds place only in the Acts of the Conciliabulum hastily assembled by Michael to pass an anathema upon the Papal Legates;[1] and in a letter addressed to the Patriarch of Antioch, where it is inserted in a passing way among the charges against the Latins.[2] But letter and Conciliabulum were both subsequent to the open avowal of the schism, and to the excommunication of Michael Cerularius, which was placed by the Legates on the altar of St. Sophia. If the insertion of the *Filioque* had been the cause of the schism, it would certainly have found

---

[1] Pseudo-Synodus Constantinop. (Labbe, t. xi., p. 1456).

[2] Michaelis Cerul. *Epist. ad Petrum Antioch.* (Cotelerius, *Mon. Eccl. Græcæ*, t. ii., pp. 142, 143. Lutetiæ Parisiorum, 1681).

a prominent place in the letter of the Patriarch to the Bishop of Trani. It is true that the Greeks commonly attribute the breach under Cerularius to that addition; but they can give us no proof of their assertion. The addition of the *Filioque* was not considered as involving the Latins in the guilt of heresy. Balsamon, who first ventured to call us heretics, was censured for doing so by the Greeks themselves.[1] And again, even Mr. Ffoulkes confesses that with exception of Michael Cerularius and his party, the excommunication of the Papal Legates did not affect the rest of the citizens, the Court, and the Emperor, who remained orthodox,[2] and four years after, intercourse was resumed between the East and the West; the Popes, especially Alexander II., held communication with Constantinople through their apocrisiarii, and nevertheless not a word was said on the addition of the word *Filioque*, no protest whatever was made by the Greeks against the Latins for their having violated the Decrees of the Synods of Ephesus and Chalcedon. The truth is that but for the management used by Photius and Cerularius, with their adherents, this famous addition would have attracted no notice whatever in the East.

If the addition of the word *Filioque* into the Creed of Nicæa served the Greeks as a pretext for schism, it is untrue that the adoption of the False Decretals had any influence. We hardly understand Mr. Ffoulkes when he says that "he is not aware that any demur to this conclusion in theory can be raised." How is it possible

---

[1] See Allatius, *De Perpetua Consensione Eccl. Occ. atque Orientalis*, l. ii., cap. ix., n. 3, p. 618, seq. Edit. Coloniæ.

[2] *Christendom's Divisions*, pt. ii., ch. ii., p. 78, seq.

that the adoption of the False Decretals could be the cause of the Greek schism? Let us compare the dates. The compilation of the forged Decretals, according to the most learned critics, such as Hinschius, cannot have been furnished before the year 853.[1] Photius seized the Patriarchal see of Constantinople in 858, and was deposed by Pope Nicholas in 863. Now it is generally admitted that Pope Nicholas at that time had no knowledge whatever of the Isidorian forgery, and much less had given credit to it; it is even doubtful whether he did not die without having paid any attention whatever to the Collection. It is clear, then, that in the year 867, when Photius assembled his Synod and published his Encyclic, the Roman See had given no ground for suspecting it of the intention of "allowing the primitive Code of the Church to be stealthily supplanted by a new Code based upon forgeries," but had constantly appealed to the true authentic Canons of the Church, and to them alone, as the valid binding ecclesiastical law. Mr. Ffoulkes is therefore wholly mistaken in attributing the Greek schism to the False Decretals, "accepted by the Popes without examination, and made binding upon others by violence." Between the death of Photius and the time of Michael Cerularius no use was made by Popes of the Isidorian forgeries, except that, as we said before, a single passage is quoted once only by each of two Popes, Hadrian II. and Stephen V. And this silence, as is well remarked by Dr. Denzinger, proves that the Popes could never have seen the whole Collection, which otherwise they would

[1] Hinschius, *Decretales*, pt. iv., sec. 20, cap. i., p. clxxxiii., seq.

have frequently quoted.[1] And if we examine the particular passages quoted by Hadrian and Stephen, all suspicion of fraud is still more effectually removed. The former cites from an Epistle under the name of Anterus a passage having reference to the translations of Bishops,[2] but this passage is merely an extract from the genuine Canon xxvii. of the Fourth Council of Carthage,[3] which, therefore, was received into the law of the Eastern Church when the Council *in Trullo* adopted all the legislation of the various Synods of Carthage.[4] The use made of the False Decretals by Pope Stephen V. is confined to the historical statement that the Canons of Nicæa were seventy in number; this is quoted by him from the spurious letter of St. Athanasius to Pope Mark.[5] It may be observed, in passing, that this imposture came to the West from the East, which part of the Church was always notoriously most fertile in forgeries. The Pseudo-Donation of Constantine was first alleged by Leo IX. in his answer to Michael Cerularius.[6] But at this time Michael was in open schism, and the Donation contains nothing in favour of the Papal authority over the East, beyond the state-

---

[1] *Ecloge et Epicrisis*, sec. ii. (In Migne, *PP. LL.*, t. cxxx., p. xiii.).

[2] *Epist.* xxxii. *ad Synodum Duziacensem* (Labbe, t. x., p. 437).

[3] *Statuta Eccl. Antiquæ*, Can. xxvii. (Bruns, *Can. Conc.*, pt. i., p. 144). Even Blondellus confessed it in his *Pseudo-Isidorus et Turrianus vapulantes*, p. 279. Genevæ, 1628.

[4] Conc. Trullanum, Can. ii. (Pitra, *Jur. Eccl. Græc. Hist. et Monumenta*, t. ii., p. 22).

[5] *Epist. Stephani V. ad Luythobium Episc.* (In *Ivonis Decreto*, pt. iv., cap. 232. Migne, *PP. LL.*, t. clxi., p. 314).

[6] *Epist.* i. *Leonis IX. ad Michaelem Cerul. Patr.* (Labbe, t. xi., p. 1327).

ment of the jurisdiction of the Pope over all Patriarchs. The Donation is a public recognition of this authority, the existence of which is clearly demonstrated by Leo IX. from the Gospel promises made to St. Peter. Leo's quotation, therefore, cannot be supposed to have exercised any influence whatever upon the Eastern schism ; and in truth, Mr. Ffoulkes has confessed, in his work on *Christendom's Divisions*, that the primacy of the Popes by divine right was not disputed in the voluminous correspondence between the authors of the Greek schism and the Popes.[1] Nay, as we remarked above, Photius himself had solemnly acknowledged the divine authority of the Pope ; and he, as well as Michael Cerularius, in their list of charges against the Latins, never objected to their acknowledging the universal and supreme authority of the Roman See. Moreover, Michael Cerularius, in the Synod held by him in Constantinople, when he anathematised the Papal Legates, not only abstained from any word against the Roman Pontiff, but also endeavoured to impugn the authority of the Legates, by representing that they had not come from Rome, nor received their mission from the Pope, but from his enemy, Argyrus ; and he asserted that their Papal Letters were mere forgeries of the same Argyrus.[2] It is plain then that the authority of the Roman Pontiff was felt in the Eastern Church ; and that the schismatic Patriarch feared lest the respect and veneration which was still found among the Greek Bishops for the Pope would overthrow his iniquitous designs. The mistake of

[1] *Christendom's Divisions*, pt. ii., ch. i., pp. 4, 45.
[2] Pseudo-Synodus Const. (Labbe, t. xi., p. 1461).

Mr. Ffoulkes, and of many other writers upon the same subject, arises from not discriminating between the causes of the schism and the causes which led the schismatics subsequently to persist in their separation from Rome. We agree with the view held by most Protestant writers, that the supreme power of the Pope is at present the chief subject of controversy between the Greeks and other heretical and schismatical bodies; but this is the consequence, and not the cause of disunion. In ancient times the Papal authority was fully acknowledged by the Patriarchs and Bishops of the East, as is proved by very many documents which might be cited, and by the entire absence of any repudiation of the authority claimed.ABundant proof of what we say will be found elsewhere.[1] It will be enough to mention the formulary drawn up by Pope Hormisdas, and signed by such Eastern Bishops as returned to Catholic unity after the Acacian schism; which formula was also signed by all the Prelates present at the Eighth General Council after the deposition of Photius. The wording of this document is such as clearly to show that the claim of authority is based upon the promises made by Christ Himself; and we find a clear statement of the obligation incumbent upon every Christian of being joined to the Apostolic See, that he may rest upon the sure rock and unshaken foundation of the Catholic religion,[2] while it is expressly declared that all who are not in communion with the Roman Church are cut off from the

---

[1] *The Supreme Authority of the Pope*, secs. iv., v., p. 81, seq.
[2] In Denzinger, *Enchiridion Symb. et Defin.*, p. 50. Edit. 1865.

communion of the Church Universal.[1] Thus, in the sixth and ninth centuries, the Eastern Church pronounced by anticipation a solemn sentence of condemnation against the schismatic followers of Michael Cerularius.

XIII.

The guilt of this schism is much enhanced at the present day, when its followers persist in obstinately disregarding the decrees of union adopted at the Fourth Lateran Council, at the Second of Lyons, and at the Council of Florence. Mr. Ffoulkes feels that some defence is necessary for his Greek friends upon this point; and accordingly he does his best to throw discredit upon the proceedings at Florence by heaping up calumnies upon the Council, and upon the great Pope Eugenius IV., who was its president. He says that "of all Councils that ever were held, there never was one in which hypocrisy, duplicity, and worldly motives played a more conspicuous or disgraceful part."[2] He tells us that by the use of such means the Council of Basle was outwitted, and Florence named as the place to which the Greeks should come; that the galleys of the Pope outstripped the galleys of the Council, and bore the Greeks in triumph from Constantinople to a town in the centre of Italy, where the Pope was all-powerful. He continues in the same

---

[1] L. c. "Sequestratos a communione Ecclesiæ Catholicæ, idest, non consentientes Sedi Apostolicæ."
[2] *The Church's Creed*, p. 20.

strain for two more pages, pointing out the promises of soldiers and galleys made by the Pope to the Emperor in the course of the Council, as if they were means calculated to induce him to accept the Decrees of the Council; with much more to the same effect. It is not our purpose to examine accurately the history which Mr. Ffoulkes has detailed at some length in his *Christendom's Divisions*, and which he has summed up in three pages of his pamphlet. To do so would carry us far beyond our own limits, and it is not necessary to undertake the task. A few remarks, however, must be made upon the subject.

As to the words—"hypocrisy, duplicity, and worldly motives," it is enough to say that not a particle of evidence is forthcoming in support of the charge which they convey. Mr. Ffoulkes continues that, "Basle was outwitted and Florence named as the place to which the Greeks should come." The explanation of these words is to be found in the second part of his *Christendom's Divisions*.[1] There he informs us that the Twenty-fifth Session of Basle, which named Florence for the meeting of the Council, was not passed by the majority of the Fathers, but by the minority. But who has ever denied this? At the same time, Mr. Ffoulkes does not tell us what is well known, that the *majority* of that Session was composed of the dregs of the Council, of simple country Priests, and of servants of the Prelates, who had been admitted into the Congregations with the right of voting,[2] while

[1] Ch. vii., p. 332, seq.
[2] "Hæc factio ex vili plebe magna ex parte constabat, quamvis ducem haberet Cardinalem Arelatensem. . . . Adversæ factionis

only one Cardinal and a few Bishops were at their head. On the other hand, the minority comprehended all the best and wisest members of the Synod. In it there were the most influential Prelates, and what is more important, the Papal Legates, who presided, and with whom the Greek ambassadors solemnly professed agreement. Had Mr. Ffoulkes explained what kind of people formed the majority of Basle on the 7th of May, 1437, the weakness of his case would have been more apparent.

But he adds another "scandalous preliminary"—that the seal of the Council was surreptitiously affixed to the Decree of the minority, which was carried to Pope Eugenius and sanctioned by him. We remark that there is a contradiction between the accounts given on the subject in the Acts of the Council published by Patricius, and in the statement of Panormitanus. Patricius does not conceal the nature of the Decree of the majority of Basle, as Mr. Ffoulkes thinks, but he relates that Cardinal Cervantes, Nicholas Tedeschi, Archbishop of Palermo, and the Bishop of Burgos, to whom the seal of the Council had been intrusted,[1] affixed it also to the Decree of the minority.[2] It may easily be understood that this act was received with a burst of indignation by the *soi-disant* majority, and condemned in the Twenty-sixth and Thirty-second Sessions, especially

capita clericos undique cogunt; veniunt turmatim ex vicinis oppidis et civitatibus Sacerdotes, et qui etiam in urbe Patribus serviebant plerique et in Ecclesia togati convenientes jussa præstabant suffragia" (Patricius, *Hist. Conc. Basil. et Florent.*, cap. liv. In Labbe t. xviii., pp. 1352, 1353).

[1] Mansi, *Suppl. ad Conc. Veneto-Labbeana*, t. v., p. 1.
[2] Patricius, Op. cit., cap. lv. (l. c., p. 1354).

after the assent of the Pope had been given to the Decree of the minority when the Council of Basle was definitively transferred to Ferrara. But whatever was the course which, under the necessity of the circumstances, the minority adopted, the right of affixing the seal of the Council to the Decree belonged to the minority, not only on account of the character of the Prelates and Cardinals whom it comprehended, but principally because it was headed by the Papal Legates. The Council, indeed, represents the Church: the Church however is not a number of Clergymen, but a compact and organised body under the headship of the Vicar of Christ. Now, the Council constitutes a body when it adheres to the Pope through his Legates; then it represents the Church and commands respect. In the Synod of Basle the majority was only a number of Clergymen of the lowest rank, but the minority formed a body with their lawful Head; therefore it had title to represent the Church. But, moreover, Mr. Ffoulkes appears to believe that the translation of the Council of Basle to Ferrara, rests on the authority of the Decree of the Twenty-fifth Session of Basle. This is a mistake. The translation of the Council from Basle to Ferrara, and from that town to Florence and finally to Rome, was due only to the authority of Pope Eugenius, who decreed it. The Pope alone has right to transfer an Ecumenical Council, as he alone has the right to assemble it. This is Catholic doctrine, laid down most explicitly by Leo X. in the Bull *Pastor Æternus* in the Fifth General Council of Lateran.[1]

---

[1] "Solum Rom. Pontificem pro tempore existentem, tanquam auctoritatem super omnia concilia habentem tam conciliorum in-

Now these are the "scandalous preliminaries" of the Council of Florence of which our writer speaks, these are the artifices by which the Synod of Basle was outwitted. The Greeks were desirous to be again united with the Catholic Church; ambassadors had been sent by the Emperor and the Patriarch of Constantinople to Pope Eugenius and the Synod of Basle, in order to settle the principal conditions of the union. They asked for a place where the Eastern and the Western Churches could meet to arrange the long-expected union, but they protested against the choice of Avignon, Basle, or the Principality of Savoy. They insisted on a town in Italy being selected, to which their countrymen could have ready access; and they gave their consent when Pope Eugenius proposed that the meeting of the Greeks and the Latins should take place in some Italian city;[1] they protested that they would never have assented if Basle or Avignon, or any city of Savoy, had been suggested. The majority at Basle were fully aware of this determination of the Greeks; but they refused their own concurrence with the arrangement for no other reason than that the towns of central Italy were not hostile to Pope Eugenius, whose authority they were ever bent on undermining. These

dicendorum, transferendorum ac dissolvendorum plenum jus ac potestatem habere, nedum ex sacræ Scripturæ testimonio, dictis S. Patrum ac aliorum Rom. Pontificum etiam, prædecessorum nostrorum, sacrorumque canonum decretis, sed proprio etiam eorumque conciliorum confessione manifeste constat" (In Denzinger, Op. cit., n. 622, pp. 219, 220).

[1] The protest of the Greek ambassadors is referred to by Pope Eugenius in his Bull of confirmation of the Decree of the minority of Basle (Labbe, t. xviii., *Conc. Flor.*, pt. i., n. iv., p. 853, seq.).

Prelates, therefore, did not hesitate to do what they could to frustrate the hopes entertained of a speedy suppression of the schism, in order to gratify their passionate hostility against the Roman Pontiff. Here we have a real scandal, which, however, was far from involving the whole Church; for the majority at Basle, as we have seen, no way represented the Clergy of Christendom. But Mr. Ffoulkes is forced to take a different view, and to throw all the blame on the truly wise and honest minority who, headed by the Papal Legates, voted in favour of the adoption of the place named by the Pope himself, and to which the Greeks had assented, as offering the best hope of effecting a permanent reconciliation.

Moreover, Mr. Ffoulkes complains that the galleys of the Pope outstripped the galleys of the Council of Basle, and conveyed the Greeks in triumph to a town in the centre of Italy. This is true—but what of it? Everything was done in accordance with the Decree mentioned by the Pope and admitted by the Greek ambassadors, who had explicitly declared that they would recognise as a lawful Council those of the assembly at Basle who took part with the Papal Legates.[1] Florence had been appointed by the Papal constitution as the place where the General Council should be held, and this place was afterwards, by the same authority, changed to Ferrara; after this, the Fathers of Basle had no right to interfere with the destination of the galleys which were to convey the Greeks. And whither did the Fathers of Basle intend to convey the Byzantine Emperor and his Prelates?

[1] See Raynald, *Annales Eccl.*, ad an. 1437.

To a place against which they had protested, and to which they had repeatedly declared they would never go. And, moreover, it was impossible that Eugenius could permit that the Greeks, while anxious for union, should fall into the hands of men who were themselves actually in rebellion, and on the point of breaking the unity of the Church by a new schism. This is the vital question with which Mr. Ffoulkes ought to grapple; compared with this, the details are of little importance.

Next let us examine the kind of bargain which, if Mr. Ffoulkes is to be believed, Pope Eugenius made in the Council of Florence. The statements of Mr. Ffoulkes in this part are studiously adapted to mislead. Our author says: "Between John Palaeologus and Eugenius, it was a barter of temporal and spiritual gains from first to last.... The more sailors and soldiers the Pope promised, the greater submission the Emperor engaged to extort from his Bishops to the teaching of the Latin Church. Three Cardinals solemnly notified to the Emperor what succours he might expect from the Pope when the union of the Churches had been accomplished, just as had succeeded in getting all his Bishpos but one to declare for it," &c.[1] This is very different from the statement in the Greek Acts, where we read that "the Emperor, seeing that the negotiations for the ecclesiastical reunion were going on, applied himself to State affairs" (τὰ πραγματικά).[2] On that account, he entrusted the Bishop Rhuteneas with a mission of

---

[1] *The Church's Creed*, p. 21; *Christendom's Divisions*, pt. ii., ch. vii., p. 348.

[2] Acta Græca Conc. Florentini, Sess. xxv. (Labbe, t. xviii., p. 496).

negotiation with the Pope. But Eugenius sent the Bishop back to the Emperor with three Cardinals, who notified to him what the Pope was determined to do in behalf of the Greek empire. Their promises pleased the Emperor, who ordered that they should be confirmed by public instruments, and authentic copies deposited in Venice, Genoa, and Florence.[1] The Emperor was encompassed by the enemies of the Christian name, and was threatened with the loss of the remainder of his States; we cannot then blame him if he applied to the Pope to know what succours he might expect now that the Greeks were on the point of returning to friendly terms with the Latins. Nor can we blame Pope Eugenius because he was generous in his promises to the Greeks, whom he hoped soon to embrace as reconciled children returning after a long separation from their Father. The common-sense of men refuses to call such a transaction "a barter of temporal and spiritual gains."

But Mr. Ffoulkes, summing up in his pamphlet what he has already said in his larger work, goes on : "When the union was imminent, the Emperor said, 'The time draws near; we must be thinking of our departure.' The Pope replied, 'I have seen to it already, and will see to it. Meanwhile, take this paper from me, and when you have read it, let me have your reply.' *This was the definition*," continues Mr. Ffoulkes ; "not indeed in the precise shape in which it passed; but ships and money were to be forthcoming when it was signed."[2] Now let us turn to examine the authentic Acts of

[1] Acta Græca Conc. Florentini, Sess. xxv. (l. c., p. 497).
[2] *The Church's Creed*, p. 21.

the Synod. After the exemplary and happy death of the Patriarch of Constantinople, the Greek Emperor assembled his Prelates in order that, the question being settled as to the doctrine of the Procession of the Holy Ghost, the other doctrines might be discussed in which the Greeks seemed to be at variance with the Latins, and that thus a perfect and lasting union might be concluded. Although the Cardinals were at first unwilling to enter into argument on all these controverted points, yet they yielded to the wish of the Emperor.[1] And though the Prince was anxious that these questions should be discussed, he was obviously not very sanguine that the scheme of reunion would succeed ; perhaps he was discouraged by the evil spirit shown by Mark of Ephesus, who remained throughout obstinate in schism. However this may be, the Emperor listened to two discourses on the primacy of the Pope, and then said that no further discussion was needed ; that the time of his return to Constantinople had arrived; and that he could remain no longer in Florence. Then the Pope replied: "I have seen already, and I will see to it. I sent a captain in good time to prepare the galleys ; and I will provide and have ready whatever is needed for the return."[2] And he assured the Emperor that at all events, even in the case that no reunion should be made, the provision for his safe return would be scrupulously attended to, and that therefore on this account there was no reason for anxiety.[3] After

---

[1] Acta Græca Conc. Flor., Sess. xxv. (Labbe, t. xviii., p. 508, seq.).
[2] *Ibid.* (l. c., p. 509).
[3] Acta Latina Conc. Flor., Coll. xxii., n. vii. (Labbe, L c., p. 1162).

this assurance had been given to the Emperor, the Pope presented to him the sketch of the formula of union, entreating him to examine it, and propose his objections, if any. The Emperor was very unwilling to take the paper into his hands; and had not his Prelates pressed him to comply with the Pope's wishes, he would have persisted in his refusal, and let the union fall to the ground. But after he had examined the Articles in company with his own Bishops, they openly declared that they agreed with each of them without any reserve, and they urged their master to accomplish the work of union. Nevertheless, he seemed unwilling to do so.[1]

Mr. Ffoulkes tells us that his blood curdled as he transcribed the account of this business from the Acts of the Council. Let us see whether there is anything to account for the strong feeling which led to this result. We deny that there is any appearance of barter between the Pope and the Emperor in this transaction. The Articles offered to the Emperor by Pope Eugenius and Cardinal Julian are exactly what had already been laid down in the Convention between the former and the Synod of Basle in the Nineteenth Session, and confirmed by a Decree in the Twenty-fourth;[2] and to which "Eugenius was pledged likewise," as Mr. Ffoulkes himself has remarked in his *Christendom's Divisions*.[3] If those terms of agreement had been concluded four years before, they could not become matter for a barter between the Greek Emperor and the Pope when the

[1] Acta Græca Conc. Flor. (l. c., p. 512).
[2] In Labbe, t. xvii., pp. 308, 334, seq.
[3] *Christendom's Divisions*, pt. ii., ch. vii., p. 348, and ch. vi., p. 323.

Decree of Union was to be signed; especially as, union or not union, the promises made of securing the safe return of the Emperor were already binding upon the Pope. Therefore they could not have any connection whatever with the Decree of Union; and consequently they could not be the subject of a barter of temporal and spiritual gains. Moreover, the argument of Mr. Ffoulkes is in the familiar shape of *Post hoc ergo propter hoc*. Because, forsooth, the Pope places the Decree of Union in the hands of the Emperor after having assured him that the terms agreed to for his return would be faithfully kept; therefore, the agreement to the definition of faith is to be referred to a bargain! The Pope, before making any mention of the galleys, had said to the Emperor that the doctrine of Papal primacy being now satisfactorily explained, nothing remained to be done except to sign the Definition of Faith and the Decree of Ecclesiastical Union.[1] But the Emperor declining to do this on the pretext of being anxious for his return, the Pope explained away his difficulty by reminding him of the terms of the agreement; and afterwards returning to his own main point, presented to the Emperor the copy of the Decree, the signature of which would accomplish the union. Finally, long before this interview between the Pope and the Emperor, the Eastern Bishops to whom God had manifested the truth,[2] had pressed the latter much for the union, and went so far as to declare to him that should his Imperial Majesty refuse to take part, they would make the union by themselves. The Acts say that the

---

[1] Acta Græca Conc. Flor. (l. c., p. 509).
[2] Acta Lat. Conc. Flor., Coll. xxii., n. ii. (Labbe, l. c., p. 1146).

Emperor was afraid when he heard this; and began from that time to devote himself more effectually to the affairs of the union.[1] If afterwards he again became cold and indifferent to the union, he would not have been brought back to his early eagerness by the promises of a few ships for his return, of which he was secure, whether or not the union were concluded.

We have gone into this matter at some length, not at all as if the authority of the Council of Florence in any way depended upon it, but to afford the reader a sample of the false colouring given to events by Mr. Ffoulkes in his endeavour to justify the conduct of the Greeks, and to asperse the character of Pope Eugenius.[2]

[1] Acta Græca Conc. Flor., Sess. xxv. (Labbe, l. c., p. 485).

[2] Mr. Ffoulkes is amazed at seeing that Pope Eugenius, while occupied with the Council, found time to attend to military expeditions against some "chieftains of some rival factions, as Nicholas Piccinino, Francis Sforza," &c. Mr. Ffoulkes, when writing this, must have forgotten that Pope Eugenius, as Pius IX., was not only the Supreme Ruler of the Church, but also the King of the Roman States. That kingdom is intrusted to the Pope, as an heirloom of the Papacy, that he may govern it, and transmit it in its integrity to his successor. The Pope then is in duty bound to defend it against invaders, and repel them by spiritual and temporal weapons. Therefore, as Pius IX. has zouaves to provide for, and his territory to preserve intact, so Eugenius IV. and the rest of his predecessors and successors were bound to defend the Papal States against ambitious assailants. If Pope Eugenius, like many others of his predecessors and successors, employed Bishops and Cardinals to command his armies, it should be remarked that each age has its own customs; and, moreover, the defence of the Papal territory has always been regarded as a sacred thing, and the cause of the Church. Nevertheless, we do not intend here to write the apology of Pope Eugenius, or of any other Popes, in the question of their military expeditions. Although the Pope is infallible in his authentic teaching in the Church, he is not infallible nor impeccable in his civil and political administration. But Mr. Ffoulkes commits a

The Greeks rejected the authority of the Council, and refused compliance with the Act of Union; and this new schism at least cannot be excused from the character of open heresy. In the Synod of Florence, the Universal Church was really represented by the Eastern and Western Prelates, and headed by the Pope in person, with his Cardinals. The assembly sanctioned as articles of faith the Procession of the Holy Ghost from the Father and the Son; they defined the divine supremacy of the Pope in the Universal Church; they declared him to be the Vicar of Christ, the Head of the whole Church, and the Father and Teacher of all Christians, the Shepherd and the Ruler of the Universal Church. The Latins have faithfully retained these

twofold mistake when he asserts, first, that Eugenius IV. condescended to aid the Greeks, when he could inform Europe that they had conformed to the Roman rite, in his Encyclic of Jan. 1, 1442; and, secondly, when he states that the uppermost thought of the Pope was Hungary, not Constantinople. As to the first assertion, it is quite a fabrication. Eugenius IV. had already solemnly declared to all the Church what the conditions had been of the union restored between the Greeks and the Latins; and he refers to the Decree of Union, where everything is expressed in detail (See for instance *Epist. ad omnes Fideles.* Labbe, t. xviii., p. 1199). But what document can be alleged to prove that Eugenius in 1441 obtained from the Greeks an entire conformity to the Latin rite? In the Encyclic mentioned by Mr. Ffoulkes, the "ritum R. Ecclesiæ assumpserunt" must be understood in accordance with the Decree of Union enacted in the Synod of Florence. With respect to the other assertion of Mr. Ffoulkes, we content ourselves with remarking that the object of the organisation of the Crusade was not only to save Hungary, but all Christianity, from the Turks, and the army of Ladislaus was at Varna in order to check at that particular place the forces of Amurath, and shield Constantinople; but misfortune, or want of military precaution, or both at one time, caused one of the greatest defeats ever sustained by Christian arms.

dogmas since the time of the Council of Florence, as they had always done before. The Greeks, after full and free discussion of the dogmas, in private and in public, had agreed with them; they had signed the confession with willingness and satisfaction (ἀρχικὸς ὑπέγραψα); the authentic parchments with their autographs still exist, as irrefragable proofs of their disloyalty. In the course of the following year, the new Patriarch Metrophanes, by an Encyclic letter, announced to all the world the reunion of the Greek and Latin Churches, mentioning at the same time the doctrines defined in the Decree of Reconciliation.[1] About three years after this (1443), the three Patriarchs of Alexandria, Antioch, and Jerusalem, met in Synod in order to anathematise Metrophanes, with all those who still adhered to the union of Florence.[2] In Constantinople indeed, the Clergy was more faithful to the union on account of the virtuous efforts of the two Catholic Patriarchs, Metrophanes and Gregory his successor, who most steadily resisted the open and secret enemies of the dogmatic profession of Florence; all the efforts of the Metropolitan of Ephesus had failed to establish a schismatical party in the capital. But finally the corruption of the people, the demoralisation of the Monks and the Clergy, the weakness of the Government on the eve of its total overthrow, and the powerful influence of the Turks, cast down every barrier which stood in the way of the overflowing waves of schism

[1] The text of the Patriarch's circular may be seen in the work of Mr. Pitzipios, *L'Eglise Orientale*, pts. ii., iii., ch. iv., p. 47, seq. Romæ, 1855.
[2] In Mansi, *Suppl. Conc.*, t. v., p. 247, seq.

and heresy.[1] The Greeks condemned again not only their union with the Latins, but also the dogmas of the faith defined at Florence, which they had for several years professed. It is then evident that they are not only schismatics, but truly heretics. A schism, according to the teaching of the Fathers, cannot exist for long without heresy, how much less a schism brought into being after a union solemnly sanctioned in an Ecumenical Council, and by which defined dogmas of the faith were impiously rejected. Really, the only controversy which can be said to be in dispute now between the Greek schismatics and Catholics, is on the infallibility of the Church in its Ecumenical Councils. Before the time of Photius, many heresies had been expelled from the Eastern Church by the Decrees of General Councils; in all these questions the Roman Church was always found on the side of truth and primitive tradition, and was a sure guide in the search for the Apostolic doctrine. And subsequently to the rise of the schismatical Patriarch, the errors propagated by him and his followers were condemned again and again at Constantinople, Lyons, Rome, and Florence; and the decisions of these Universal Synods still always justified the wisdom and faith of the Roman Church. The Roman Catholic Church has been ever unchangeable in its doctrine; the Greeks have often contradicted themselves, frequently turning back to teach the errors which they had once anathematised; they have repeatedly retracted their charges against the Church of Rome and rejection of the Papal authority, and they

[1] See Leo Allatius, *De Eccl. Occ. et Orient. Perpetua Consensione*, l. iii., cap. v., seq., p. 959, seq.

are unable to cite any General Council in justification of their peculiar doctrines. If then the Church of Christ is really infallible, the Church of Rome must be the Church of Christ. Infallibility cannot be separated from truth, and truth is never changeable. The Greeks have constantly changed their doctrines and their professions of faith; they cannot then have any claim to the infallibility of the Church; infallibility remains the attribute of the Roman Catholic Church alone; and the infallible voices of Lyons and Florence condemn Photius and Cerularius as schismatics and rebels.

XIV.

LET us conclude. Mr. Ffoulkes, long before the publication of his last pamphlet, had imbibed a most erroneous idea of the constitution of the Church, its members, and its Head. He had already asserted, as an incontrovertible truth, that the Church of the Fathers was a Church "without any distinctions of precedence amongst its members outside the sanctuary, without any supreme head in or out of the sanctuary but One, Who is there worshipped in faith as ever present." Nay, he maintained that this is by far the loftiest and most evangelical idea that can be formed of the Church.[1] He conceived the primitive Church as a number of isolated communities confined to their chief towns, or scattered up and down some remote province, without

[1] *Christendom's Divisions*, pt. i., sec. 15, p. 35, seq. London, 1865.

any communion between them. He ascribed their gradual connection to a course of events which gradually formed one chain of the Churches, first of a single province and afterwards of the entire known world.[1] But Mr. Ffoulkes never conceived the existence of an organic union in the Church, nor did he see, in the particular Churches headed by their Bishops, so many living members of the Universal Church; he saw nothing but so many independent communities "associated by federal ties."[2] Nay, the Bishops, according to Mr. Ffoulkes, had only a delegated power from their own dioceses, and they were bound to confer with the representatives of other Churches for their mutual interests. The institution of Metropolitans and of Patriarchs is also represented by him as the result of accidental arrangements.[3] Mr. Ffoulkes did not believe that the authority of the Pope himself had any other origin in the Church. ".Could it have been otherwise," he says, "than a mere question of time to delegate to the Pope the same executive powers over Christendom generally, that had been delegated to the Metropolitans over provincial, and to Patriarchs over diocesan Churches?"[4] But at the same time he remarks that "had Christianity never encountered a world-wide empire at its birth, but only a number of insignificant and detached kingdoms or republics, it is quite possible that the idea of a supreme earthly head of the Church

[1] *Christendom's Divisions*, sec. 6, p. 13, and sec. 16, p. 37.
[2] In this manner he represented the union of the Church of England to the Catholic Church (*Ibid.*, sec. 87, p. 216).
[3] *Ibid.*, secs. 6, 7, pp. 14, 15.
[4] *Ibid.*, sec. 8, p. 19.

would never have occurred at all to its professing members."[1] Then he adds that "the Church's second stage towards monarchy had been actually attained before the conversion of Constantine,"[2] because "the headship of Emperors is a thing that has been tried and laid aside; what therefore remains but that of the Pope?"[3] Nevertheless, he points out, as "a fact of prime importance in ecclesiastical history comparatively unnoticed, and which should be written in largest characters, that what are called Ecumenical Councils *originated*, not with the Apostles or their successors, but with the first Christian Emperor and his successors."[4]

Every one who knows the merest elements of Catholic doctrine must perceive that the principles expressed by Mr. Ffoulkes at the time of the publication of his first part on *Christendom's Divisions* have struck at the very root of the faith, and are a tissue of errors and heresies. Nevertheless, up to that time Mr. Ffoulkes still preserved some principles, which, though in logical contradiction with the many that we have mentioned, are essential to the whole of the Catholic economy, and showed that a remnant of the old Catholic faith was left in him. He maintained that "Christendom, *to exist in all lands*, and to be *maintained in corporate unity*, must of necessity be constituted under a single head."[5] Moreover, in a letter published at that time in the *Dublin Review*,[6] he stated explicitly that he held "the Papacy to be of divine

---

[1] *Christendom's Divisions*, sec. 16, p. 37.
[2] *Ibid.*, sec. 7, p. 16.
[3] *Ibid.*, sec. 15, note 65, p. 35.
[4] *Ibid.*, sec. 8, p. 17.
[5] *Ibid.*, sec. 14, p. 35; sec. 89, p. 226, seq.
[6] *Dublin Review*, vol. v., New Series, n. ix., 1865, p. 140.

institution, and he interpreted our Lord's words to St. Peter—'I say unto thee that thou art Peter,' &c., literally and unequivocally, as conferring upon him and his successors those prerogatives which are implied in it." And he adds—"The Church in communion with the Pope is the Catholic Church in unbroken unity now, as in times past." But Mr. Ffoulkes could not long continue to hold these two principles conscientiously, and he has since made it manifest to all who care to attend to the matter, that these two principles were nothing but the whited stone hiding the rottenness within the sepulchre. The unity of which Mr. Ffoulkes spoke in the above passage was not the vital unity of the Catholic Church under the successor of St. Peter; in fact he states, in the very same paragraph, that "the Church of England alone, and the bodies that sprang from it, have any real coherence or vitality, and they are exceptions, destined perhaps to play an important part in any future schemes for reunion of the whole Church."[1] On the other side, he admits that "for the first three centuries or more, the power of the Pope remained in suspense." But he adds that "Christ foresaw that His Church would desire a visible earthly head. He therefore fore-ordained and foretold St. Peter as the Apostle from whose successors that visible head was to be supplied."[2] That is to say, according to the view of Mr. Ffoulkes, the institution of Papacy did not enter in the divine plan of the constitution of the Church, but as a matter of condescension to people

---

[1] *Christendom's Divisions*, pt. i., sec. 14, p. 34.
[2] Letter of Mr. Ffoulkes in the *Dublin Review*, l. c., pp. 140, 141.

who, after three or more centuries, would, like the Jews, ask for a King. And that act of condescension was not conceded, says Mr. Ffoulkes, without reproof on the part of God in the cases alike of Israel and of the Church.[1] Notwithstanding this, Mr. Ffoulkes, after four years more of study and investigation, has given up the remnant which he had retained of Catholic doctrine. If previously he believed the Papacy to be a divine institution, he now believes it to be a contrivance brought about by fraud and force. If he had once thought the Papacy to be necessary for the unity of the Church, he now thinks that its power has grown and spread, to the dismemberment and destruction of the world at large. Therefore he deprecates the *principle of a supreme earthly potentate* in the Universal Church, and demands that Rome be confined to the original bounds of her Patriarchate. He had professed before that the Catholic Church was the Church in communion with the Pope in unbroken unity, therefore he ranked the Church of the East and that of England in the Church of Christ, from which he excluded Nestorians, Eutychians, Monothelites, and other such heretics; but he had not openly said that these two Churches were portions of the Church One and Catholic. Consequently he considered unanswerable the charge brought by the late Archdeacon Wilberforce against the Church of England, that the West had no right at all to legislate for itself. Now, however, that wall of division has fallen, in the opinion of Mr. Ffoulkes, and its rubbish has been swept away by the new doctrines which have dawned on his mind. He does not see

[1] *Christendom's Divisions*, pt. i., sec. 15, p. 36.

that anything is needed for being in communion with the Universal Church beyond the profession of the Nicene Creed.[1] And since the Church of England and the Eastern Church agree in fully admitting the Nicene Creed, it is to be concluded that they have all the conditions requisite for being true portions of the Church of Christ One and Catholic. Mr. Ffoulkes openly professes this doctrine. "The Greek Church," he says, "is as much a part of the Catholic Church as the Latin, although separated for the time being from the Pope."[2] And in his last pamphlet, which we have been examining, he asserts that "there are Churches *forming part of the Catholic Church* which are, and have been for ages, out of communion with their See (of the Pope)."[3] Therefore he considers the doctrine of the visible Headship of the Church under Christ as an ideal picture, not representing the actually existing Church. And he believes that at present there is no part of Christendom seriously purposing to call itself the Catholic Church in these days.[4]

Thus, if we seek to discover the leading idea of the pamphlet, we shall not be able to gather it from the title-page. Mr. Ffoulkes wrote his pamphlet as an apology for his own real interior apostacy (be it material or formal) from the doctrines of the Roman Catholic Church. He is a High Churchman again, and consistently advocates the system of the Church of Three Branches. And this explains why he labours so much

---

[1] *The Church's Creed*, p. 65.
[2] *Christendom's Divisions*, pt. ii., ch. x., p. 566.
[3] *The Church's Creed*, p. 43.
[4] *Ibid.*, p. 45.

to overthrow the Scriptural and historical Catholic idea of the Papacy, representing it as the offspring of force and forgery. To do this was necessary from his point of view, in order to justify the separation of the Greek and Anglican Churches from the See of Rome. On the other side, he, like most Anglicans, regards communion as unnecessary to the Catholicity of each of the two detached Churches, and assuming as granted the validity of the Anglican orders, he states that "the administration of the Christian Sacraments might be frequented with profit outside the pale of the Roman communion,"[1] that is to say, in the Anglican Church as well as in the ·Roman Catholic Church; because "plain Christians," he says, "may traverse the world with no other passport to the Sacraments of the Church in all lands than the Nicene Creed."[2] Therefore, the general subjects of which Mr. Ffoulkes treated in his pamphlet were Papacy and schism; his principal scope was that of giving some stability to the position of the Anglican Church and of his Protestant friends, tossed to and fro and carried about with every wind of doctrine. The title of his pamphlet does not convey its general argument and its aim. The author was prompted in his choice of a title by the soreness resulting from the two excellent recent publications of Archbishop Manning,[3] which showed the falsity of the pretensions of the English Establishment. He does not conceal the trouble and anxiety which these publications caused him, and he

---

[1] *The Church's Creed*, l. c.
[2] *Ibid.*, p. 66.
[3] *The Crown in Council on the "Essays and Reviews." The Convocation and the Crown in Council.* London, 1864.

comes forward as a champion of the Anglican communion with the purpose of retorting against the Catholic Church the difficulty urged by his adversary against the Anglican Establishment, and of strengthening the position of the latter. Mr. Ffoulkes imagined that the insertion of the *Filioque* in the Nicene Creed furnished him with a fair retort against the Archbishop, and he entered the more readily into the controversy because he hoped that, while defending the English Church, he would also be able to make out a case in justification of the Eastern schism. But as we said, the discussion on the addition of the word *Filioque*, as well as on the Procession of the Holy Ghost from the Son, are not the principal part of Mr. Ffoulkes' pamphlet, nor do they represent its real and practical scope. The title of the present answer corresponds with the view here taken of the real bearing of the Letter of Mr. Ffoulkes.

The lamentable shipwreck of Mr. Ffoulkes is due to the want of elementary theological principles to guide him amidst his historical studies. He should have known that the unity which Christ gave to His Church is a vital unity; that He, the Divine Saviour, organised the Church as a visible Body, animated with invisible *charismata*, which form the divine principle of its humano-divine operations; that consequently He appointed Peter to be its visible Head, that its organisation might be complete. But the Church, being constructed after the likeness of a body, could not be for three centuries bereft of his head, though it was not necessary that its supreme ruler should exercise his full authority in its first age, as was proper in later times. If Mr. Ffoulkes had conceived the idea of Church unity as it is held by all Catholics, he would not have been led to believe that Papacy was the result of forgery and force. Moreover, if Church unity is a vital and organic unity, no one can actually belong to the body of the Church unless he is in connection with the whole, and under the influx of the Head. A morbid growth of flesh, or a putrefied limb, as long as it is thoroughly connected with the body, belongs to and is an actual part of it; but as soon as it is cut off, it no longer belongs to the body, and it no more forms any portion of it. The Church of England and the Church of the East were both once portions of the whole Church of Christ, and by being united to the body of the Church they were under the supreme authority of the Pontiff, and consequently they partook of the vitality of the whole. Once separated from that unity they were no longer portions of the Church of Christ, which is One and Universal. In the Eastern communion, where Order was preserved, we may find Sacraments, but no administration of them with proper Jurisdiction, for the Sacraments were entrusted by Christ to the administration of His Church; but the Eastern communion is not the Church of Christ, nor any portion of it. The practice of Christian virtues, even resting on supernatural principles, may truly be found both among many of the Anglican Establishment as well as of the Eastern communion, and the reason is manifest: first, because it is of faith that the agency of actual grace is at work even beyond the limits of the Church of Christ; and secondly, because even among those who are separated from the Church many individuals are found who, being in good faith, are not formally detached from vital unity, and consequently they may possess sanctifying grace with all the habits of supernatural virtues. But that the Holy Ghost, with His *charismata*, can be possessed either by individuals who are *formally* alien to the Church's visible communion, or Churches with Pastors and Bishops emancipated from connection with the See of Rome and submission to it, is a heretical proposition, which no Catholic can hold without giving up his Catholic profession. Either, then, Mr. Ffoulkes intended in his late pamphlet to give formal notice to all whom it might concern that he had ceased to be a Catholic, or he has given public proof of ignorance of the elements of Catholic doctrine.

Works by
FATHERS of the SOCIETY OF JESUS.

Rev. PAUL BOTTALLA.

Lately published, cloth, 6s.

THE POPE AND THE CHURCH, considered in their mutual relations with reference to the errors of the High Church Party in England.

PART I.—THE SUPREME AUTHORITY OF THE POPE.

⁂ The Second Volume is preparing.

LONDON : BURNS, OATES, AND COMPANY.

Rev. PAUL BOTTALLA.

Lately published, price 3s. 6d.

POPE HONORIUS BEFORE THE TRIBUNAL OF REASON AND HISTORY.

LONDON: BURNS, OATES, AND COMPANY.

Rev. GEORGE TICKELL.

Just published, cloth elegant, 7s. 6d.

THE LIFE OF BLESSED MARGARET MARY. With some account of the Devotion to the Sacred Heart.

LONDON : BURNS, OATES, AND COMPANY.

FATHER PONLEVOY.

Just published, cloth, 9s.

THE LIFE OF FATHER DE RAVIGNAN, OF THE SOCIETY OF JESUS. Translated at St. Beuno's College, North Wales.

DUBLIN : W. B. KELLY, GRAFTON STREET.

Works by Fathers of the Society of Jesus.

REV. HENRY J. COLERIDGE.

Lately published, cloth, 7s. 6d. ; *calf limp,* 10s. 6d.

VITA VITÆ NOSTRÆ MEDITANTIBUS PROPOSITA.
A Harmony of the Latin Gospels in parallel columns.

This work has been compiled for the purpose of putting the several accounts of our Lord's life, action, and teaching, side by side in a handy form, available either for study or meditation, and also for exhibiting the order and succession of the events of the Gospel history, according to the great divisions into which that history most naturally falls. It is also intended, though complete in itself, to form the basis of a future commentary on the narrative of our Lord's life. It is divided into seven parts, the first of which embraces the birth and infancy of our Lord ; the second begins His public life, and ends with His retirement before His persecutors soon after the second pasch ; the third contains the whole period of the early training of the Apostles, from the first selection of the twelve to the confession of St. Peter ; the fourth begins with the change of character in our Lord's teaching after that confession, consisting chiefly in the clear promulgation of the doctrine of the Cross, and the prediction of the approaching Passion, and carries on the narrative to the eve of Palm Sunday ; the fifth and sixth contain the events of Holy Week and the history of the Passion ; while the seventh puts together the various accounts of the Resurrection, the Forty Days, the Ascension, and the Descent of the Holy Ghost on the Church at the Day of Pentecost. The principles which have been followed in the arrangement of the harmony are explained in a short preface.

LONDON: BURNS, OATES, AND COMPANY.

Published occasionally in Parts. Price 2s 6d.

SERMONS BY FATHERS OF THE SOCIETY OF JESUS.

Now ready,

PART I.—THE LATTER DAYS.
Four Sermons by Rev. Henry J. Coleridge.

THE TEMPTATIONS OF OUR LORD.
Four Sermons by Rev. F. Hathaway.

PART II.—THE ANGELUS BELL.
Five Lectures by Rev. P. Gallwey.

THE INFANCY OF OUR LORD.
Three Sermons by Rev. T. B. Parkinson.

In October,

PART III.—MISCELLANEOUS SERMONS
By Various Authors.

LONDON: BURNS, OATES, AND CO., 17, PORTMAN STREET, W.